2014

6/14

Push Back!

How to Take a Stand Against Groupthink, Bullies, Agitators, and Professional Manipulators

D0881900

B. K. Eakman

Skyhorse Publishing

Skyhorse Publishing books may be purchased in bulk at special discounts for sales promotion, corporate gifts, fund-raising, or educational purposes. Special editions can also be created to specifications. For details, contact the Special Sales Department, Skyhorse Publishing, 307 West 36th Street, 11th Floor, New York, NY 10018 or info@skyhorsepublishing.com.

Skyhorse® and Skyhorse Publishing® are registered trademarks of Skyhorse Publishing, Inc.®, a Delaware corporation.

www.skyhorsepublishing.com

10 9 8 7 6 5 4 3 2 1

Library of Congress Cataloging-in-Publication Data is available on file.

ISBN: 978-1-62636-418-9

Printed in the United States of America

Contents

2   Contents

BEGINNER COURSE—PROVOCATION AND CONSENSUS

Introduction

It's tough today to be a traditionalist, constitutionalist or even the generic "conservative" in America's ever more left-leaning, bureaucratic political scene. Even the trusty dictionary and thesaurus are against you, characterizing "conservative" in negatives: "old-fashioned," "unadventurous," "fearful of change," "inflexible," "reactionary."

Most Americans have been conditioned—through their schools, the media and the "popular" culture—to crave *acceptance* and *comfort* more than to cherish the liberties identified in the US Constitution.

Anthony Daniels, a physician and former prison doctor in Britain, who also writes under a pen name in America, recently observed that people don't necessarily *want* to be free; they'd rather be comfortable. His comment was this:

> "It is a mistake . . . to assume that all people want to be free, in the sense of the American pioneers. I think they much prefer to be comfortable; as the establishment of welfare states almost everywhere . . . has shown. [T]he greatest of all freedoms, the one that people want more than any other, is freedom *from* responsibility and consequences."

In order to be completely *comfortable*, special privileges emerge for preferred groups and bogus government payouts. The populace becomes increasingly dependent, regimented and regulated. A bureaucracy grows by being tasked with ever more oversight duties, onsite inspections and, finally, enforcement.

I ought to know; I was once among those bureaucracies.

Bureaucrats have powerful incentives to enlarge departments and enforce regulations. Soon you have a *government* that "creates jobs." Once *that* begins to sound normal, the nation is in trouble.

Counter-Strategy Earns Successful Results

I noticed this evolution of enlarging government while I was still a classroom teacher, and again later, working for several federal agencies. I learned a lot, and started reading more on the political strategies of countries that had skidded into, rather than directly ordering up, their fully regimented societies. I found my first golden opportunity to use this new-found knowledge in a mandatory sexual-harassment/ AIDS-awareness workshop for employees at the federal agency where I worked. Everyone had to sign up for one of three days.

As most of us expected (including the liberal staffers, which today usually comprises a majority), it was all about political correctness. Since the workshop was required, most employees were anxious to show that they were sensitive <u>and</u> not prejudiced. So, my colleagues smiled and preened, even though they were miffed at having been pulled away from their desks—mostly piled with "make work." Even so, leaving the busywork unfinished would have affected their employee evaluations.

The lady who served as the moderator began by asking: "What pops into your head when I say: 'AIDS', 'HIV', 'sexual orientation'?" We were all supposed to call out something.

Then she dimmed the lights and showed a short film featuring interviews with homosexuals and others—they may have been actors— all of whom, of course, decried "homophobia" and went on to express incredulity that something so "normal" could cause a person to be ostracized. Afterward, the moderator worked, without much success, to generate discussion, and then turned to the topic of how one could *not* get AIDS or HIV from the fellow in the next cubicle, or by using the same bathroom, etc.—which was only minimally accurate, as long as one doesn't accidentally take in a bodily fluid, such as splash-ups from drinking faucets and whatnot.

What neither my colleagues, nor the moderator herself, knew was that there was someone in the room who not only understood we weren't getting the whole picture, but also had researched and written on consensus-building, the kind where psychological manipulation is a sucker's game.

After listening to the p.c. spiel for half an hour, I waved my hand: "Excuse me, I have a question."

Now, this was music to the moderator's ears because she *thought* that she might be starting to connect with her unwilling participants. So, I said:

"I think all of us here know the risk of catching AIDS or HIV from the person in an adjacent office or bathroom is minimal. That's *not* what concerns us. What many of us *are* concerned about is the compromised immune systems of folks who indulge in risky sexual behavior, individuals who go on to get strains of pneumonia, tuberculosis and other contagious diseases that are resistant to antibiotics. What materials have you brought us to address this issue?"

The moderator was flummoxed. She never expected the question, had no literature, and no snappy retort. I yawned and stretched, then said: "Well, if there's nothing in your arsenal that addresses <u>real</u> concerns like this, I think we're done here."

I got up and proceeded to walk out, **whereupon everybody else followed me out of the room—including the liberals.**

This is how you co-opt phony consensus meetings, and get others, including weaker colleagues, even those representing other political views, to join you.

But wait: What, exactly, *did* I do?

Actually, several techniques were at work here, even though it all appeared very smooth:

- First, I didn't give the moderator anything to arouse suspicion, either through something I said or my prior body language, until *she un*intentionally provided an opening (which I figured she would, eventually). So, she had no means of shutting me out.
- Secondly, I didn't get distracted by her effort to create a "we" mentality with her little opening gambit of "what pops into your head. . .?" In fact, I used the tactic on her!
- Thirdly, I didn't refer to myself; I used terms like "many of us" and "we," making it difficult for the facilitator to ostracize me.
- Finally, I affected a calm, laid back, non-confrontational, even a bored, demeanor, which drew in even my liberal colleagues.

These techniques are grounded in the axioms and rules of psych war that we will be studying and practicing in this course.

If you're reading this text, *you're* not looking to be comfortable. You expect to counter your smug opposition. You recognize the absolute necessity of taking the battle to the adversary. Some leftist tenets have become embedded in the Republican Party, in fiscally conservative groups, and a few religious organizations, too.

Make no mistake: We didn't win the Cold War. We lost it. The Left has been busy since the 1970s taking America down. They're regrouping in places like Vietnam which recently began offering free university-level education in July 2013 to those applicants at state universities who agree to study the works of the approved pantheon of orthodox communist thinkers, and is hoping to attract more students globally. This goes beyond the requirement for all students to take courses in Marxist-Leninism.

Many countries in South America have seen a resurgence of old Soviet-era dictatorships. The Left has become really good at provocation and agitation. Someone even better has to deal with them.

America is going down an eerily familiar politically correct path, complete with penalties for noncompliance. Thus, *you* are a rarity, if you are willing to push back. Dissention is tantamount to being "uncooperative" and "argumentative," both of which have been determined by "experts" to be signs of mental disturbance. To be honest, I don't know if traditionalists and constitutionalists actually have the numbers anymore. But if we stick to counter-strategies that work, numbers *per se* make no difference, as we shall discover in this course.

Starting Point

Where *does* one start? In your neighborhoods, in your schools and houses of worship, in town meetings, task forces, focus groups, local campaigns and curriculum committees. You must *shut down the bullies*—nearly all paid to come in from the outside and "facilitate" local meetings or task forces under the cover of chairing, or maybe "moderating," a discussion to make sure the "consensus" goes a certain way. Their bottom line is always to increase reliance on government at local, county, regional, state and, finally, the federal level—the classic description of *creeping socialism.*

Dependency upon government typically begins under the cover of "a good cause," and from there, it moves along subtly to mandatory compliance. The underlying justification for certain programs and attitude-changes creates a vicious cycle: more local, state, regional and federal spending. Once governments at all levels start depending upon what is known in political circles as "pass-through *federal* dollars" to get the job done, there follows an accumulating public debt from which, eventually, there is no escape.

For example, many Republican lawmakers—suddenly sensitive to the growing public disdain for ObamaCare, with its increasing list of previously unnoticed taxes (such as for medical devices like X-ray machines and oxygen tanks)—are in a quandary. They know that their constituencies are addicted to related government programs, like Medicaid! So, in March 2013, some Republican legislators in Congress made a show of rejecting any expansion of the program under ObamaCare, while simultaneously applying backroom influence to allow for an extension of—guess what?—Medicaid benefits!

This stands in stark contrast to the values endorsed by the Founders of our nation in the Declaration of Independence, the Constitution and Bill of Rights—concepts like self-sufficiency, self-reliance, self-discipline and self-determination—ideals that formed the cornerstones of the American experiment in *self*-government. But "self" is now the operative term that no longer dare speak its name!

Are You a "Troublemaker"?

Many of you, no doubt, have had the frustrating experience of being treated as a "troublemaker" as soon as you raise a concern about a policy, proposal, or school curriculum? Sometimes you wind up ostracized when all you wanted was to inject another viewpoint.

Unfortunately, most laypersons—which sometimes includes even legislators—don't realize they're dealing with well-trained provocateurs the minute they set foot in the room with folks who are chairing a meeting. These chairpersons frequently have an ulterior motive.

To have your view heard and taken seriously, you must know, first, how to recognize psychological manipulation. You must be able to reframe a debate, take it *away* from your adversary, and argue the issues you and your colleagues want to discuss, and not get sidetracked into your opponent's agenda. To do this requires mastering certain principles of argument, then applying them <u>in</u> a group setting, *under pressure.*

The AIDS/sex awareness workshop opened a window for me: I discovered I had a knack for this, and many of you will find that you do as well. Even if you don't, you can subtly support those who do.

SECTION 1

Agents of Change and "Marginalization"

For reasons you will understand shortly, *it's easier to control a group than it is to control an individual.* Now, that may seem strange, but it's actually the reason behind attempts to collectivize participants in focus groups, committees, etc.

Unethical facilitators—those with ulterior motives—will try to maneuver you toward groupthink instead of "I think." That's the first giveaway that you are dealing with a professional manipulator. Manipulators go by several other labels, too.

You may be familiar with manipulator acting as:
- change agents
- provocateurs
- agitators
- community organizers
- technical assistants
- in-person assisters

The differences are minor, but involve big bucks. City officials, for example, may award millions in grant monies to for-hire services to "help" local residents qualify for benefits and subsidies under a particular federal or state program that is being pushed. Take D.C. Health Link, for instance, as reported by Tom Howell, Jr., in the *Washington Times* August 14, 2013. This organization was awarded sums between $80,000 and $400,000 to send out "in-person assisters" to "raise awareness" of and urge participation in certain reforms associated with ObamaCare. They are "touting the Affordable Care Act at local events . . . and ramping up out-reach in libraries, partnering businesses and houses of worship. Each assister receive[s] about thirty hours of training."

"Change Agent" Recruitment

Assisters are relatively low on the totem pole of professional manipulators. Change agents and hard-core agitators get considerably more in the way of recruitment and training.

Professional recruitment for advanced training in group facilitation and all manner of alternative forms of group manipulation is responsible for getting you (and, for that matter, your kids) caught up in peer pressure and group-think.

Manipulation can start off as nothing more than slick ads aimed at glamorizing trashy pop artists, and getting kids (and even grown-ups!) to copy the "look" of hookers and pimps. The kind of culture rot being thrown at children virtually assures sexual experimentation among pre-adolescents, who are in the hypersensitive, giggly stage on matters relating to their bodies and the bathroom.

But everyone, from educators to vigilant citizens' groups, is at risk today. Professional recruiters are busily seeking out and training "community organizers" and "agents of change."

Take, for example, the likes of the American Planning Association (APA). The APA is one of several, large, third-party front groups. Many are twenty-somethings recruited from liberal colleges and universities— young people who have been "vetted" surreptitiously for their liberal-leftist viewpoints in their dormitories and college classrooms. The question for recruiters is whether a potential candidate can perform well in unfamiliar settings to change attitudes and secure consensus where there may be pockets of deep resistance. Recruiters take their cue from hostile, foreign spycraft: identifying politically driven students at top universities; adding in ambition and high IQs; stroking their egos and exploiting both their vulnerabilities, emotional needs, and idealism.

Most recruiters are well-connected, which allows them to clear the way (or block) a college-level pupil's career path. In other words, recruiters are, in essence, "handlers." The differences in the sophistication of the various manipulator labels are detailed even further in the "post-graduate" section of this book.

For now, just recognize that any unwary group of "concerned citizens" can actually *help* one of these entities pull the rug out from under every participant. You can be isolated, ridiculed, ostracized, and finally overwhelmed. The good news is that you can shut down the process, or even do the same in reverse, providing you know how.

Honest and Dishonest Debates

Most of us are caught up in the idea that the best way to get through to an adversary is in a heart-to-heart, fact-based discussion. That's true only if people are honestly debating an issue as equals. It's not true if the debate is dishonest. If a provocateur can generate a mob mentality, and get it to work for him, *control of the agenda* is usually assured. So there's a rule for you: *Never let the other fellow control the debate, or agenda.*

Manipulation Begins Early

The foregoing discussion of recruitment is a major reason why so many formerly rigorous, academic tests have deviated into psychological assessment ("screening)" packages, featuring data-mining and profiling. Most of the information collected is secured only insofar as it is labeled "confidential"—a term which, in a legal sense, translates as "need to know," not "anonymous."

Contrary to popular belief, the US Department of Education (DoEd), its state arms, and most of their contractors and grantees are disseminating assessments (often under the cover of "standardized testing"). They all are well aware of the differences between an *assessment* and a *test*, and know how to avoid legal action. According to two of the DoEd's primary agencies, the National Council of Education Statistics (NCES), in its voluminous May 2002 publication (the text is updated every few years), and the North Central Regional Educational Laboratory (one of several federal educational research/oversight facilities scattered about), here is a sampling of definitions clarifying this

- "An assessment is any systematic procedure for obtaining information from tests and other sources that can be used to draw inferences about characteristics of people, objects, or programs."
- "Assessment is the process of gathering information about children in order to make decisions about their education. Teachers obtain useful information about children's knowledge, skills, and progress

by observing, documenting, and reviewing children's work over time . . . ."

- "Assessment is the process of observing, recording and otherwise documenting . . . ."
- "Assessment involves the multiple steps of collecting data on a child's development and learning . . . ."

Moreover, the education establishment knows how to skirt the legal minefields associated with "testing" by using the cover of "screening."

Among the culprits is the huge teacher's union, the National Education Association. It taps promising candidates both in the undergraduate college classroom and at the post-graduate level for special courses at its National Training Lab in Bethel, Maine. Such facilities serve as "boot camps" to teach potential operatives the techniques of intimidating the opposition. NTL "graduates" go into the classroom and impose various radical ideas on *children*; whereas outfits like the APA send their newly minted recruits out to local communities posing as *facilitators*—which people take to mean "moderators of a discussion."

Trained recruits work to deftly pit factions of a community, citizens' group, committee or even classrooms full of students against one another, to make the favored side of an issue (the one they are hired to promote) appear "sensible" and any opposing factions seem out-of-touch. This is how the facilitator assumes control of the **psychological environment.**

Provocation Basics

The basic technique in all cases of group manipulation is to *heighten* peer pressure (or, as adults would call it, "social pressure") until the group functions as a "we" (or "us") mentality. This is not a setting in which every person is an individual and every individual's input counts. What provocateurs get out of *groupthink*, is a "mob mentality"—the antithesis of what our Founding Fathers had in mind when they created our nation's form of government.

Once this occurs, ideas can be planted that go against 2000 years of civilization. Both children and adults will accept outrageous and/ or unworkable proposals for no other reason than that the *group* finds them fashionable, which is helped along by media hype.

Of course, children are typically sitting ducks for hard-core manipulation tactics. But adults are in trouble, too.

Most folks are ill-equipped to stand up for their principles, much less teach their kids to do so. We fear being censured and insulted. When we feel cornered, we may sound hysterical, raise our voices, and ensure our doom. So essentially, the provocateur gets the *group* to do the dirty work. This is part of what will later be described as the Delphi Technique, but it is true of all professional agitation and manipulation.

You will want to disrupt, or better yet, *pre-empt* the establishment of a facilitator's psychologically controlled environment. You will need some rules for this game, so that you can counter the techniques as you go, *and get others in the group to help you (like I did in the sexual harassment/ AIDS awareness workshop, whether they understand what you are doing or not)*. Moreover, you have to beat the provocateur at his (or her) own game, and typically you will have no backup.

Who's in control?

- It is easier to control a group than to control a single individual.
- Whoever controls the debate, or agenda, usually wins.
- Pre-empt the psychologically controlled environment to avoid being victimized.

Psych War Is Not a Negotiation

Many of the principles you will be studying here are take-offs on an ancient Chinese text, *The Art of War*, thought to have been written around 476 BC. This little book has received renewed attention lately, but too few really understand the axioms well enough to counter them.

Four Axioms of Psych War

- A resistance movement is not run according to rules of etiquette.
- Those skilled in war subdue the enemy without physical battle.
- Deception and surprise are two key principles of battle.
- Confuse the enemy's leaders—"if possible, drive them mad," then forge ahead.

So, demoralization of the enemy was a high priority, even in 476 BC. Trained opponents will try to demoralize you; that's the *point* of all psychological agitation and provocation. Professional manipulators may simply try to flatter you into accepting a new agenda.

Most of the time, your antagonists will be a relatively small, radical core of smooth-talkers who have been trained to overwhelm a larger body of people, often for-hire. Sometimes it takes only one person, the guy or gal *you* thought was a moderator or a negotiator, to engineer a consensus nobody wants. Whereas a real moderator is supposed to keep a meeting "on message" and moving along, and a real negotiator works to pull two parties together to resolve a specific dispute, an unethical manipulator's mission is part of a larger offensive against those holding to traditional values, especially when it concerns standards of morality and culture.

Psych War's Effect on Social Issues and Culture

Particularly since the 2012 election, you have probably noticed many high-profile Republicans backing away from traditional cultural and social issues, in hopes of getting more people behind fiscal and defense concerns. But the truth is that once social values are trampled and the culture is trashed, the country slowly loses the rest, too.

Many adults today don't remember, but in 1973 we had radical campus groups with silly names like Students Against Capitalist Exploitation, the Symbionese Liberation Army, and of course, the Black Panthers and Students for a Democratic Society. Members and their less adventuresome hangers-on, initiated the trend of wearing dungarees to class, dyed their hair purple, and made "smoking weed" fashionable. They claimed to be forging "a new consciousness." Playing at being revolutionaries, they carried signs against "imperialists" (who, in many cases were their own successful fathers, men who hired the employees that grew both jobs and the economy in general). Their radicalized youngsters, the first-wave Baby Boomers, however, devoured books by now-forgotten foreign agitators like Herbert Marcuse, and popularized the term "pigs" for "police." In essence, they became overgrown adolescents with nothing to otherwise occupy their time—and certainly much less tuition to pay than today's students. They claimed to be "committed to social change," to "distributing wealth equitably," and to replacing bosses and corporate heads with "average workers."

The buzz-term "workers," of course, is used for nearly every form of endeavor now, but in the early 1960s it implied having neither a college degree nor job experience—borrowing from the claptrap of Communist revolutionaries. The idea was to keep the so-called "rich" from benefiting from the country's largesse, especially from receiving "perks" (special privileges), when _lower_-level employees were barely making ends meet.

Eventually, the mainstream media and universities popularized this perception like good leftists. America never recovered from that.

Beginning even in the Reagan Administration, blatantly left-wing blather began spewing forth from schools, major newspapers and Capitol Hill. The Left's entire "value neutral"-"situational ethics" mantra became intertwined with curriculum. Activities that had previously been morally unacceptable were systematically "de-stigmatized." For example, some of today's high school campuses have added a day care facility to accommodate the toddlers of teenage unwed mothers. This not only allows these young, single parents to "stay in school," but carries an implied destigmatization of illegitimacy and promiscuity.

The Latest Wrinkle in "Assessment/Screening"

The news media gives one no hint that the National Security Administration (NSA) metadata scandal exposed by Edward Snowden had its origins in the last place average citizens would ever look for it—in the nation's public schools. It came along under the cover of "testing," which, as previously indicated, was renamed "assessment." For example, some of today's high school campuses have added a day care facility to accommodate the toddlers of teenage unwed mothers. This not only allows these young, single parents to "stay in school," but carries an implied destigmatization of illegitimacy and promiscuity.

The Obama administration's Common Core of Standards (CCS) requires even more in the way of personal data collection from pupils, in addition to expensive, revamped _interactive_ computer systems, which cuts parents totally out of the loop. A side-effect is the easy potential for increased manipulation of student attitudes and values. For that reason, more accurate labels for CCS would have been the Common Core of Attitudes, or the Universal Core Political Correctness. It is linked to the newest rendition of federal reform initiatives, this time under Barack Obama's so-called "Race to the Top" initiative, which, like every "new" education initiative since the 1970s, is inextricably tied to federal strings in a typical bait-and-switch package of incentives for states to sign on to.

The new version of assessments under CCS will scrap the old method where students used a Number 2 pencil to color (or "bubble in") a response. No more computerized sheets or booklets to be physically packaged up by proctors and sent to a contractor, which fed them into a computer for tallying, tracking and storage in government systems. The new version under CCS makes the paper questionnaires of 1990s and early 2000s look like Smithsonian Museum pieces, even the old word-association tests we are all familiar with. The new versions are modeled on the Implicit Association Test (IAT)—what is known in neuroscience as "rapid cognition" screening.

Most people, never mind children, cannot comprehend the technique involved—at least not quickly enough to fake their responses. The idea, as always, is to ferret out the assessment-taker's unconscious, automatic beliefs, as opposed to those the person either consciously chooses to act upon, or maybe even *thinks* he or she believes, but for reasons of culture—nonstop exposure to films, everyday reading material, and TV—has mentally overwritten. So the test-taker winds up revealing deep-seated attitudes by way of this breakthrough association-based method.

How does a rapid-cognition technique accomplish what the older paper questionnaires could not? By programming a computer to force forcing a respondent to decide between what appear to be random associations very quickly—in milliseconds. The test-taker, especially a child, cannot remember a specific item long enough to take the particulars home. Yet, just one millisecond of time spent on marking a question or selecting a column in which to place the given word spurs the computer program to categorize the test-taker as, say, "moderately biased" toward this view or that.

The topic can be race (there is a "Race IAT," a "Work/Family IAT," and so on). The idea is to trigger unconscious associations and implicit biases about religious attitudes, nationalistic tendencies or something else in the blink of an eye. (An excellent analysis of "rapid cognition" is contained in best-selling author Malcolm Gladwell's 2005 book entitled *Blink: The Power of thinking Without Thinking*.) These instant-response, computerized assessments blow the lid off of earlier, better-known attitudinal assessments: like the *Personality Assessment Inventory* and the *Minnesota Multiphasic Personality Inventory*, and elements of these new screening devices can be adapted for everything from student assessments to job applications.

Trained facilitators and other manipulators are very familiar with this technique. Thus, the facilitators' questions thrown out at the beginning of their presentations, such as the one this author faced in the sexual harassment/AIDS workshop, asking what participants associated with various hot-button terms. This is essentially an adaptation of IAT methods, but done quickly to avoid giving you time to think about your response. Whenever thinking is discouraged, it makes you more anxious to appear cooperative—for instance, by calling out something rather than by remaining quiet and reflective. The only difference is that this adaptation of the method (i.e., talking) is not computerized—that is to say, "automated." But don't imagine for a minute that a facilitator is unfamiliar with the computerized version of this technique. They simply adapt it to community groups naïve enough to accommodate the facilitator's ploy.

Public "Conditioning"

First, you need to understand how "psychological conditioning" enters into the mix. Take the following example: Three little words, such as "national security threat," repeated *ad nauseam* in various venues and formats, can serve to condition mainstream America and have us salivating like Ivan Pavlov's dogs. The expression has been drilled into our collective subconscious since Sept. 11, 2001. That's why most of the media and lawmakers bought in. It is also why these entities failed to question the administration's mass surveillance and drone initiatives vigorously, and then to connect the dots to our metadata-collection systems. It was only a matter of time before somebody like Edward Snowden, NSA-contractor-turned-whistleblower/traitor (depending on your viewpoint), revealed the existence an out-of-control domestic spying apparatus, growing out of real needs relating to human intelligence on foreign terrorism.

So, how does "conditioning" relate to group manipulation? Just this: Whenever we run up against an expressions like "national security threat," we are now fully acclimated—which effectively shuts down all complaints relating to "probable cause" or anything else. Soon, nearly the entire population loses the will to protest misuse of authority. Such a public mindset not only gives new powers to a ruling elite, but on a smaller scale helps facilitators and provocateurs "sell" (or "impose") their agenda, winning over the skeptics and small groups. Why? Because the constant browbeating —known in the vernacular as "perception management"—tends to shut down (or "freeze") normal responses. Government has reacted predictably: In typical knee-jerk fashion, law enforcement is eyeing unmanned aerial surveillance to ensure against future Boston Marathon-type events. This will have the side-effect of unleashing a torrent of unwarranted spying for *political* purposes.

Need proof? Take the ubiquitous network of spy-cameras, which have become standard operating procedure for every major event, whether they are billed as traffic cameras, speed cameras, red-light cameras, safety cameras or (more honestly) revenue cameras. Even the animal rights group, People for the Ethical Treatment of Animals (PETA), which sets an unusually high standard for its definition of "abuse" (such as horse-racing), is considering the purchase of "drones" in a plan to watch hunters and farmers who might fall under PETA's radical interpretation of "saving animals."

With the technological capability to make unmanned aerial vehicles (the popular expression "drones" comes from sci-fi films) smaller, faster, affordable and even lethal, a new dimension (literally) has been added. A convention August 13, 2013, at the Washington Convention Center in the Nation's Capital, hosted by the sector's top trade group, the Association for Unmanned Vehicle Systems International (AUVSI), showcased a copious array of newly minted varieties, some small enough to fit on the corner of a coffee table or even in your hand. You can find many pictured online in the *Washington Times* under staff reporter Ben Wolfgang's cover story on the convention.

These news stories fly in the face of earlier reports by various journalists nationwide debunking revelations in January and February responding to allegations that some thirty thousand UAVs, armed and unarmed, were being readied for deployment over American cities in five-to-seven years. The allegations, some with photos of the facilities producing them, were carried in media outlets as varied as *Business Insider, USA Today,* United Press International, *The New American* and the American Civil Liberties Union—all with a negative, privacy-challenge spin. One story scooped the competition in 2012 by revealing that the Environmental Protection Agency was testing the use of spy planes over Iowa's and Nebraska's cattle ranches.

Moreover, the August 13 Convention turned negative perceptions about UAVs around 180 degrees, by hyping the positive aspects. By then, Snowden and NSA/metadata revelations were "old news," and the "drone" cat was out of the proverbial bag anyway.

This is how public opinion is subtly molded: The "anti" and "pro" reports are just far enough removed from each other (six months to a year), that people don't quite remember them—or maybe didn't even read both—so that a negative perception quickly becomes a positive one.

Even some journalists in the news business are considering forays into unmanned aerial surveillance—starting off, of course, with something seemingly benign, like aerial videos in the aftermath of hurricanes, tornados and other weather events. Since satellite coverage is already in use, it's not such a bizarre idea. After all, paparazzi have long used their telephoto lenses to capture celebrities surreptitiously.

The same sort of turnabout has occurred with "assessment" (psychological) testing in schools and employment applications. By 2012, few cared if even the 1974 law surrounding family privacy in schools, the Federal Educational Rights and Privacy Act (FERPA), had been essentially eliminated.

The US Department of Education is taking its cue from the Environmental Protection Agency (EPA). The EPA's plan to use aerial surveillance to catch potential polluters on ranches and farms in the Midwest mirrors other progressively heavy-handed tactics, interagency collusions, draconian interpretations of mission (e.g., *Sackett v. EPA*, 2011) and vindictive settlements. Even when the government loses—as in *Hage v. the United States*, 2010—entities like the EPA have become so powerful that, like the IRS, even in the wake of highly publicized scandals in 2013, the agency felt confident enough to indulge in fancy luncheons and plush vacations on the taxpayer's dime.

These are the kinds of things one used to hear about in Russia— places where elite rulers all had Party cards and, of course, Party perks, while the nation's average citizens jumped through endless hoops and endured long lines.

Today, US citizens spend their time similarly; the difference is that we suffer through long lines at the airport, and half-hour wait-times on the phone caught in "trees," entering one number after another in a futile attempt to reach a live human or get an answer to a simple question. We are reminded over and over that our "call may be monitored and recorded for training purposes and quality assurance." If we are fortunate enough to finally reach a live person, we are asked to repeat the same information we just punched into our telephones.

In the interim, we are urged to log onto a dot-com, where we may spend hours getting a computerized run-around, and read countless pages of text in a vain effort to settle our question or concern.

Moreover, we are now thoroughly prepped, or conditioned, for a bureaucratic, robot-like encounter. We have no energy left to complain. We are anxious to get on with things.

Inately, we know that to imagine today's high-tech electronic snooping *not* being interconnected is naïve. Surveillance cameras, "traffic" cameras, webcams, lifestyle data (like subscriptions), purchases, e-mail and telephone intercepts are only a need-to-know away from mass-cross-matching. We stand like a deer in the headlights, already unable to make a decision as to whether to fight or flee.

Fortunately, some individuals *are* able and willing to hold onto their values and attitudes—not to mention their sanity and rationality—so that they still retain the capacity to respond to events as they occur. They know when something feels "off," and say so. They come up with ideas that can circumvent problems and help save us all. That is the one hope left to Americans. Let's explore how this happens so we can make use of a more proactive mentality.

Aiding and Abetting "Mis-Information"

The numbing of normal reflexes and "brain freezes" exemplifies how a consensus can be built up so seamlessly that adults who are nevertheless too young to remember the college climate of the 1960s and '70s, today cannot turn on the TV, read a major newspaper or see a movie that does not in some way feed them the "accepted" (and *expected*) political line. Thanks also to progressive education, most of us alive today are not well enough schooled to get a sense of when we are being manipulated, lied to, or that something is out of whack.

Courses like philosophy, logic, and rhetoric used to be part and parcel of a senior high school curriculum—or at least standard college work—but these mostly disappeared in the 1970s. About the closest a student gets to such course work now is in law school, or maybe taking philosophy as a college major—a relatively rare event. Even then, such classes do not highlight academic freedom, as Americans once knew it—that is, open discussion, and learning *how* to learn.

This means that the biggest problem you face in your towns and neighborhoods are that most people don't know *how much* of what they hear and read is based on *legitimate* consensus, *how much* is hearsay, *how much* is conjecture, and *how much* is pure manipulation. Two applicable quotations come from comments made by award-winning action-thriller novelists—the late Michael Crichton (*Jurassic Park*) and the very much alive David Baldacci:

In a September 2003 speech to The Commonwealth Club, Crichton said:

> The greatest challenge facing mankind is . . . distinguishing reality from fantasy, truth from propaganda. . . . [I]n the information age (or . . . the *dis*information age), we must daily decide whether the threats we face are real, whether the solutions we are offered will do any good, whether the problems we're told exist are in fact real. . . .

Baldacci coincidentally reiterated this predicament when he penned an Author's Note to readers in 2008:

> . . . a major untruth can be established so quickly and overwhelmingly across the world that no amount of digging by anyone after the fact can make a dent in the public consciousness that it isn't actually true at all.

This is the situation we're in—whether you are talking about climate change, education, child discipline, same-sex "marriage," or national defense.

You wouldn't know from the headlines, for example, that the Earth's overall, average temperatures haven't changed in sixteen years; or that the Arctic ice has returned to what was considered normal for centuries; that hurricanes and tornadoes (labeled "monster storms" by the media) are near the lowest levels in decades; or that the general rate of rise in sea-level is neither worse nor better than in 1900. You would not know that *mind* and *brain* are not interchangeable terms, and therefore would not be aware that the expression "mental illness" is a capricious label given to thoughts and behaviors which can be neither medically verified nor "cured."

Such *mis*information (again, a result of "conditioning," endlessly repeated) greatly impacts the rush to invoke tough new laws and over-the-top policies under the catch-phrase "zero tolerance." It puts a Catch-22 twist on mental health *screening*, and lends legitimacy to the idea of employees spying on each other (beginning with federal workers) and reporting any activity perceived as "offensive" or "narrow-minded" to authorities. Schools encourage the same in questionnaires and surveys given to young pupils. History should have long since communicated to us the chilling ramifications of such initiatives under tyrants ranging from Hitler to Stalin. But time passes, and history glosses over certain events. So we fail to connect, say Hitler's "Brownshirts" and Communism's "Young Pioneeers" to our present situation. Most young adults couldn't even tell you what those two terms mean.

SECTION 2

"Medicalizing" Attitudes and Perceptions

What is popularly known as *consensus-building* has a dark side that makes manipulation easier than most people think. Your first run-in with a professional facilitator may be at a community meeting or in a committee debating any number of hot-button issues. Once the group disperses, you leave feeling troubled and unsure as to exactly why. Maybe you voted *for* something you went there to vote *against,* or vice-versa. Only a few hours or days later, might you realize you got "hoodwinked."

What most folks don't know is that prominent factions both inside and outside of the mental-health field have already pronounced traditionalist and conservative-sounding views *psychological aberrations.* Some people's first encounter with this was during the widely publicized 2013 IRS scandal. Moreover, something you may have said, magazines you subscribe to, or even giveaway body language can serve as a warning signal to a facilitator as to how to handle a group or individual long before an issue is placed "on the table" for discussion. Those supporting certain views may have been marginalized days or even months ago.

How can this happen? Who does that sort of thing?

Traditionalism and Constitutionalism as "Illnesses"

If you don't believe that conservative political attitudes are being "medicalized," you need to read Chris Mooney's book, *The Republican Brain.* The term "Republican" here is generic, as it is clear from the book that author Chris Mooney really means those who self-identify as "conservatives," or who lean that way. These appear to include traditionalists, constitutionalists, the independent-minded, privacy advocates and, in particular, serious adherents of Judeo-Christian faiths. In that vein, "conservatives" are characterized by Mooney and hundreds of like-minded colleagues as *closed-minded, resistant to change, rigid* and *intolerant;* whereas individuals who self-identify as "liberal" and adhere to politically popular opinions are branded as *liberating, open, optimistic* and even *courageous*:

"[L]iberals consistently score higher on a personality measure called 'openness to experience,' one of the 'Big Five' personality traits, which are easily assessed through standard questionnaires," said Mooney.

What standard questionnaires is the author talking about? Those assessment/mental-health screening and surveying instruments we discussed earlier on.

Mooney is hardly alone. The current emphasis on what is called "cross-cultural" psychology with a politically motivated spin has permeated teacher training institutions and the media with the notion that traditional American values are not only damaging on a global scale, but *deranged* and *disturbed*. Individualists are given the label of *loner*—which, we are told, is dangerous— as it signifies being a misfit, an eccentric, a maverick. (If you doubt this, type the word "individualist" into a document, highlight it and go to the synonym list. Do the same thing with "conservative." You'll be in for a shock.)

"Self-reliance," "self-sufficient" individualist are further portrayed as ". . . less exploratory, less in need of change—and more conscientious . . . ."

Now, you'd think being conscientious was a good thing, right? But conscientiousness has somehow gotten a bad rap because, of all things, it indicates "an appreciation of order and structure" in daily life.

Who knew?

Well, if you think about it, this dovetails with the new, standard definition of conservatism as "resistance to change" and "uncertainty avoidance," as quoted in the list below.

To further validate this position, other "experts" have weighed in; among them:

- Robert McCrae, who performs studies on personality. He says: "Open people everywhere tend to have more liberal values."
- Social psychologist Arie Kruglanski (University of Maryland) finds that traditionalists (which includes biblical Judeo-Christians and individualists) are in "need [of] closure." He echoes the mantra about there being a strong relationship between liberalism and openness.
- Canada's University of Manitoba associate professor of psychology, Robert Altemeyer, even developed a Right Wing Authoritarian ("RWA") Scale, through mental-"health" screening (that's a part of those "health" questionnaires, social studies surveys, and even standardized

assessments kids get). Altemeyer works to detect individuals harboring conservative "mental illnesses." Where are the liberal mental illnesses, or even atheist mental illnesses? Apparently, he can't find any.

- The University of London published so-called "findings" that conservatives have an enlarged "fear" area in their brains, with *smaller areas associated with courage and optimism.*
- A 2005 taxpayer-funded, joint "study" out of the National Institute of Mental Health and the National Science Foundation, attributes notions about morality and individualism to *"dogmatism," "uncertainty avoidance,"* and *"mental rigidity"*—all terms having longstanding *negative* connotations, which are passed along to the public in the media.

Consequently, it is hardly surprising that today's K–12 schools have converted much of their academic testing to attitudinal assessment. What they are assessing is the child's "belief system" in an effort to launch a new field called ***preventative psychiatry***—of which psychotropic drugs are becoming an integral part, ostensibly aimed at heading off mental disorders in a sort of "preemptive strike."

Beyond individual personality traits, there are family values, such as those related to monogamy and sexual intimacy. The prevailing, mainstream wisdom is that improved medical technologies connected to birth control, abortion and morning-after emergency contraception renders such values moot.

Today's non-stop exposure to, and accommodation of, a promiscuous "hook-up" culture is taking young women (and even men) to a place most of them really don't want to go—to a semi-permanent state of instability, where sex is a performance sport. Like other sports, the players are compared and critiqued. A poor "exhibition" is improved with "performance enhancement drugs," just like in baseball, except there are no legal penalties involved.

This kind of thinking is so far removed from love and romance and intimacy that there are a whole lot of people who don't want to go there. Yet, every magazine you open, nearly every TV drama, movie and sit-com you see demands it. Tenderness and affection have devolved into an obsessive mix of sexual aerobics, erotic clothing (such as T-shirts for little girls, adorned with the message caption "FUTURE PORN STAR"), and "trash-talk" passed off as music.

So, these manipulators, by whatever label, are not mere struggling human beings trying to make sense of it all. They are out to change the "game," for money, and are shaping public perceptions to *expect* insecure homes and living arrangements.

We've all seen films and read about what happens when public consensus becomes mob mentality. Some seventy years ago, Nazi Germany and the Soviet Union launched programs to, first, win over the public and make certain views popular. In other words, both Hitler and Lenin built their regimes around a consensus. Eventually it became dangerous, and finally a crime, to hold any view contrary to the Party line. This launched two successive reigns of terror throughout Europe, Soviet satellite countries and Southeast Asia for people harboring "undesirable thoughts." Again, we see today a modern adaptation: Our version of the latter is court-ordered, mandatory mental-health "counseling."

In World War II, millions of our young men shed blood on foreign soil to protect the free world from such a fate. Yet, here we are, going down exactly the same road.

Consensus vs. Compromise

To launch our study of counter-strategies, let us begin with a working definition of "consensus."

What is consensus?

- Consensus: group solidarity in sentiment and belief and/or general agreement.
- People think consensus means compromise, but what is wanted is unanimity, or uniform thinking.

Learn to recognize a real consensus from the manipulated version, and then any sort of consensus from a *compromise*. This is your best chance of figuring out whether you're in danger of being duped.

For example, you may notice someone in the midst of your group who seems sort of out-of-place—a person (or person<u>s</u>) who appear to run counter to the beliefs of everyone else; yet they somehow manage to intimidate the entire gathering. Out of the blue, they blindside you, and get everybody tongue-tied.

For example, you might find such a person at a church meeting aimed at combating a situation in which ministers suddenly face the prospect of marriage rites for same-sex couples, a church where parishioners and clergy are very traditional. A church meeting is held, and there are a few unusually animated people speaking *up* for homosexuality. Oddly, no one recognizes them—at least not from regular church attendance. Yet, they are given a forum—why? Because we've been conditioned to be open, tolerant and polite!

Yet not a single person dares to ask aloud: "Why do these loudmouths go to church _here_, with a minister and parishioners they can't possibly like?" Instead, we give these guys the floor, in the spirit of honest debate. Why are we more afraid of appearing cantankerous, narrow-minded and inflexible—all politically incorrect behaviors—than we are of a couple of agitators taking over our meeting and steering our church in an entirely different direction until today, the US Supreme Court has laid the groundwork to make any other view illegal?

Sometimes, of course, it's the moderator, the facilitator, who stacks the deck. Those outspoken oddballs at your church <u>and</u> a facilitator may actually be in cahoots, with the outbursts choreographed. It's not all that difficult.

In any case, a *consensus* generated in a pre-arranged forum like this is manipulated. It typically is taken by one of those hired facilitators or change agents we discussed in the last chapter higher-ups—such as a chief executive officer, or maybe to elected officials—and presented as "what parishioners, the community or committee really wants."

A manipulated consensus is actually *groupthink*. It is not the result of individual, thoughtful and rational analysis. But people hear the term "consensus," and fail to connect it with a mob-mentality, knee-jerk reaction. However, if you can stop the provocateur right there, with the phony consensus, you can get a *real* conversation going.

What is a manipulated consensus?

- Unethical consensus-building is dependent upon groupthink, which requires a mob mentality.
- Facilitators keep the individual from thinking for himself and encourages him (or her) to defer to the group.

A phony **consensus is essentially a collective opinion** that doesn't reflect <u>anyone's</u> opinion. Pros can pull this off as "compromise" because the collective good is viewed as superior to, *and more important than*, the individual good. "Consensus" is a stronger term, because *the pro and con viewpoints, in a groupie, collectivist mindset, no longer exist.*

The purpose of the *facilitated, unethical consensus* is to *preserve the illusion that there is lay, or community, participation* in policy-related decision-making, when in fact *there is not.*

Suppose a professional consultant is trying to get a local community to back new regulations that support dedicating a large area to a wind farm. They know they have to at least *pretend* to involve residents in the decision and have something to that effect *in writing* in case people later complain to their representatives about this typically inefficient use of large land masses.

So, what this consultant, or facilitator, does is control the "psychological environment"—something I derogatorily call "*climate control.*" This makes it easier for one side to frame the debate and keep the other from doing so. A psychologically controlled environment provides a platform from which to operate and prevents people like you from injecting an alternate viewpoint and taking back the discussion.

Climate Control

- The key to psychological manipulation is "climate control." This applies equally to a group, or an individual.
- Framing the debate is key to the keeping control of a psychological environment.

Mass Psychology and Alienation

This sets up a kind of *mass neurosis*, because people like you are sitting there scratching your head. You know the consensus isn't true. Yet, the lie is presented by "reputable" sources that are credible, and therefore believed. This leads to a psychological condition known as "cognitive dissonance," meaning an *irreconcilable conflict* has been set up—another way of "medicalizing" opinions, preferences, perceptions and viewpoints. As people become increasingly uncomfortable, they vacillate, lose their frame of reference and become alienated. People look for comfort inside their own group instead of thinking for themselves. And with that, they reveal the members of their own faction.

Alienated committee members, particularly if they comprise the backbone of a community, help the facilitator because this gets the primary resistance out of the way.

The Irreconcilable Conflict

Cognitive dissonance keeps an individual from thinking for himself and instead "defaults" to groupthink (i.e., the individual believes he needs his peers more than his principles).

Karl Marx's Theory of Alienation was that people would do almost anything to avoid ostracism or ridicule; that they could be made to *need* each other *more* than they need their principles. One of the prime Marxist-Communist sympathizers and infamous proselytizers in America, Saul D. Alinsky—his defining work was *Rules for Radicals*—was widely disseminated among college students, "community organizers" and communist sleeper agents in the 1970s. Alinsky emphasized the necessity of humiliating and marginalizing potential opponents, whether they were correct about an issue or not.

Theory of Alienation

Marx's Theory of Alienation basically states that people will do just about anything to avoid being ostracized or ridiculed—which results in alienation.

Alinsky's book was so well-funded and circulated that it gave rise to what is called the **Alinsky Method.** One way to activate this method is if the provocateur whips dissenters into a frenzy of anger, until they become so <u>out</u>raged, <u>en</u>raged, and frustrated, that they start lashing out in all directions—losing focus and in disarray.

So, understand that *professional provocateurs are not interested in any exchange of ideas.* They aren't writing well-considered discourses to each other like the Founding Fathers did in the Federalist Papers. Agitators want to "drive the opposition mad"—to cause the core group to act irrationally.

As the frustration level is turned up, eventually someone *some*where may go off the deep end. A bomb, for example, explodes at an abortion clinic. A "survivalist" holes up in a secluded area and starts shooting "trespassers." This thrills our adversaries, because then they can say that *all* people who oppose abortion for any reason at all, or who advocates smaller government, are "loners"—a "danger to themselves and others," right? No wonder we're afraid to speak out! No wonder we're getting clobbered!

Remember, this is a crash course. Professional agitators and provocateurs spend weeks, months, even years perfecting the techniques you are learning. Throwing hardball tactics back in the face of a professional is risky unless you have practiced. You may memorize *the theories and methods* but without practice you are likely to modify the techniques just enough to botch them under stress: Too much (or too little) emphasis on certain words, a telling facial expression: These can give away your hand.

SECTION 3

"Climate Control"

One problem is that most of us don't think like marketing agents. Our adversaries do. We care about integrity—the end doesn't always justify the means. The opposition doesn't. We worry that others might get hurt if we speak out. Professional agitators and provocateurs don't care. Be it magazine ads, billboards, brochures, newspaper columns, speeches, press conferences, or grant proposals, *psychological impact is vital to our opponents—not facts, not principles, and certainly not "bourgeois ideas" about right or wrong.*

Let's learn more about rigged consensus-building and how the deck can be stacked against you or a specified group.

The Delphi Technique

The Delphi Technique is a favorite of unethical activists to achieve consensus on a controversial topic or regulation. A well-trained professional will start off as everybody's pal, then go about the business of pitting one faction against the other.

The setting or type of group in which the technique is used is immaterial. The logic behind its success is that most <u>groups</u> tend to share a particular knowledge base and display a finite set of identifiable characteristics. What the provocateur must do is identify the smaller factions within the larger group. Thus, a facilitator's opening effort to ascertain everybody's knee-jerk reaction to a hot-button term! This, you may recall, is an adaptation or "rapid-cognition," which we touched on earlier, a technique which may or may not fit into a computerized format.

What these pros really do is work the group over to ensure a *predetermined outcome.* If the discussion is "facilitated" properly, all participants will emerge believing that the decision reached was *their own idea.* Only later will some realize they were duped.

As I explained at the beginning with my engineered walk-out in the mandated sexual harassment/AIDS-awareness course at a federal agency, the facilitator starts off by eliciting input from the audience. He or she forms miniature "task forces," urges participants to make lists, and so on. In going through these motions, two things happen:

1. You can't concentrate while you're making lists and listening to the facilitator, and
2. The moderator, or facilitator, is memorizing your body language and facial expressions.

Losing Your Train of Thought

A *distraction* is an effort to change the subject, or to divert people's attention from the real issue. It will remain your constant task to remember what you are really discussing.

The provocateur is trained to identify the leaders, the "loudmouths," any weak or non-committal persons, and those most likely to change sides during an argument. In short, he or she is working to *distract* you.

But first, the amiable facilitator will work to become an accepted member of the larger group. It's only later that s/he'll turn factions of the group against each other. Suddenly, s/he plays "devil's advocate," making those views that run **counter** to the pre-established outcome appear unknowledgeable, inarticulate, or dogmatic. S/he will get everybody yelling at each other until no one even remembers what they were talking about! Yes, that can really happen.

This is a highly effective strategy against parents, teachers, pupils and community groups. The "targets" rarely, if ever, realize that they are being manipulated. Even if they suspect, they generally don't know how to shut the process down.

Suppose a desired policy like "no failing grades" is placed on the table at a school policy meeting. The provocateur may utilize a "selective hearing" process so that only those questions that support the no-D's or F's policy will be placed into discussion.

Selective Hearing

If a facilitator pretends to ignore a question or comment, or simply declines to place your suggestion "on the table" for discussion, you are dealing with a "pro."

The only *opposing* arguments permitted will be those the facilitator deems helpful in *escalating tensions* later on.

Keys to Manipulation

1. Escalating Tensions
2. Distracting Individuals
3. Confusing the Issues
4. "Divide and Conquer"—i.e., getting the group to do the dirty work

---

So, if you have an opposing view, and you *suspect* this is not the preferred view, don't be taken in even if the facilitator acknowledges your suggestion. Remain on your guard.

The provocateur, still acting as a moderator, guides the discussion so that no one else assumes control. One by one, participants accept, *if* grudgingly, the no-failing-grades idea *as if it were their own,* and they will be manipulated into pressuring the rest of the group into accepting the proposition, too. Why?

Because Karl Marx's Theory of Alienation is essentially correct. Particularly those of us born since 1945 have been *conditioned* since we were schoolchildren to do almost anything to avoid being ostracized, ridiculed, or lose face with our peers. Aware that something is going wrong, and unable to explain or confront it, we react *ab*normally.

Links Between Alienation and Conditioning

Hopefuls being recruited and trained as facilitators, change agents, provocateurs and agitators learn that in order to alienate people and get them to go outside their comfort zone hinges on three capabilities: repetition, isolation, and labeling the hold-outs.

Keys to Conditioning

Repetition: The same catch-phrases heard often assures belief or acceptance.

Isolation: If people are undermined, embarrassed, or out-maneuvered enough, they'll give up or sound irrational.

Labeling: If negative markers are applied consistently to certain ideas, a majority will come to view those advocating such views as "goofy."

A good facilitator will repeat catch-phrases and buzz-terms using varied formats and contexts, enough to get you accustomed to hearing them. Isolation, of course, is just another version of alienating someone. A person who is being isolated will feel as though the facilitator and other participants are talking *around* them, not *to* them.

Labeling is tricky because, although leftists continually carp against stereotyping, the application of **implied** negative connotations, such as the terms "extreme," "extremist," "loner," or "self-styled patriot": These don't immediately come across as stereotyping. But they *do* serve to make the unwary back away from any person or idea consistently used in these contexts, as we learned from the 2013 IRS scandal.

The "pros" are good, they really are; don't underestimate them.

Also, between the computer and word of mouth, it's fairly easy today to pre-select individuals who are most likely to agree or disagree with a proposal and "pack" an audience. Participants against a facilitator-desired proposal are frequently invited, but screened ahead of time to assure that they will not be particularly articulate, or that they will sound shrill in their voice, or that they have a reputation for being unorganized in their presentations. So *don't be overly flattered* if you're asked to serve on a controversial committee or task force.

Resisting Delphi

The key to resistance lies in grabbing control of the debate, or psychological climate; keeping the real issue firmly in mind (which is harder than it sounds); avoiding giving the facilitator any goodies to work with; and determining your own viewpoint on the base issue to avoid getting railroaded into side topics (also tougher than it sounds).

The Keys to Resistance

1. Keep control of the debate (i.e., the psychological environment).
2. Determine the real issue.
3. Don't give a facilitator anything to work with until s/he reveals an agenda.
4. Decide your view and remember it.

The facilitator is, in effect, going to tell you and your group what to think *about*, and for *how long*. That's the same thing major newspapers do with their headlines—tell you what you are going to think about, and for how many days or weeks. A facilitator knows that **whoever controls the debate, controls the agenda.**

"Belief System": Key to Thought Control

The key to manipulating another person's perceptions is to alter the belief system. **A person's attitudes, taken together, comprise his belief system.**

Your "Belief System"

- A person's attitudes, worldview and outlook comprises a belief system.
- Slogans and catch-phrases tend to redefine terms you thought you knew.
- Manipulation + peer pressure + repetition = control of the psychological environment.

People typically are unaware of their belief system, as it is made up of unconscious, automatic assumptions and responses to situations built up over a lifetime. The mathematical breakdown, as shown, goes like this:

Manipulation + Peer Pressure + Repetition = Psych Control

Therefore, appealing refrains like "Smart Growth" and "urban sprawl" are coined by perception management firms, *paid for* by special interests, *pushed to* politicians, journalists and over the airwaves until deceptive concepts are viewed by most people as indisputable. Our side would do well to devise more slogans of our own. We're being out-maneuvered.

Another way facilitators engineer sea-changes of viewpoint is that they have been able to *ease* traditionalists and conservatives away from familiar ground and force them into a hypothetical environment.

Today, when you walk into a meeting, you may be hit with a *hypothetical* environment that is essentially *foreign* to your experience, but which *requires* your involvement—a game of what-would-you-do-*if.* Classic questions from a facilitator follow this mold: "Now we don't want our children to become HIV statistics, do we?"

A Hypothetical Environment

- A manipulator will distract you from how you feel personally and re-set to a "we're-all-in-this-together" motif.
- Then, the group is moved into various "what-would-we-do-if?" scenarios.

Take this example of a meeting for parents at a local school: A facilitator may take you from an environment in which parents exercise guidance and leadership by insisting upon certain standards of behavior, and lead you to a place where anything goes and kids make their own decisions.

Thus, the first part of any resistance process is to shut down the facilitator's, or provocateur's, psychological environment and create your own. Don't play the facilitator's game. Don't allow him to take you to a hypothetical, "we're-all-in-this-together" environment. There's a time for that, for example when terrorists slammed airplanes into the Twin Towers and the Pentagon. It is not the case in a meeting over report cards, same-sex "marriage" or climate change. A consensus— perhaps over mandatory auto emissions, *might* be appropriate in Pasadena, Calif., where local geographical conditions trap smog. But you are going to have to figure out, and pretty darn quick, whether this "we're-all-in-this-together" thing is legitimate, or not.

Moreover, facilitators, and any "plants" in the audience, are basically there to sell you something you don't want or need—in the form of a program, curriculum, activity, perception, or process. They are not there to help the community, school, student, or church group decide policy. They are there to get you to do what they (*or more likely their employers*) *want.*

Remember, change agents and facilitators are mainly hired out. Their establishment earns a reputation for being good at what it does and farms out its services. So, if you're sitting there thinking, "Wait a minute, this *wasn't my* idea," you may be right. One of your first tasks, before you ever walk into the meeting, is to find out who will be moderating. Don't call up and ask who the sponsor is. The secretary will just say "the school," or "the church," and so on. You want to know *who* is being paid to chair it, *who* stands to benefit and *who* the stakeholders are.

Now, facilitators will call *you* a "stakeholder" when you walk into a meeting, too. Again, the purpose is to get you and your group into a "we're-all-in-this-together" mode. But the *real* stakeholders are the facilitators' behind-the-scenes *clients*: the World Resources Institute, the Environmental Defense Fund, the Sierra Club, the Wildlife Federation, teacher unions. Is there a program they may try to sell your district or county?.

Your job is to force the facilitator to expose this agenda early on, *before he, or she, gets you to define yours*—just like I did in the sexual harassment/ AIDS workshop I mentioned at the beginning of this course.

Real Issue vs. Advertised Topic

You may, for example, find advertised, ahead of time, some theme for a meeting which later turns out to be quite different. Remember, once you sit down, the facilitator works to "feel out the group," to get a handle on where everyone is coming from. So the thing to do is stay quiet and stone-faced for a while.

After you've figured out the real issue and committed to keeping quiet, ask yourself: *What is my basic position on this issue?* Remember it. Repeat it frequently in your own mind if you have trouble shutting out the "noise."

Others, of course, will have a different view. What the facilitator wants is a *synthesis* of two opposing positions, which will be called a compromise. But the synthesis be whatever position the provocateur's boss, or *client*, wants it to be!

Let's take a proposal to get "green" initiatives started in the schools. What's the first thing you should do?

Answer: Determine the issue.

Will the issue—that is, the group's reason for meeting—be presented as a proposal to push global warming to eight-year-olds? Probably not. It will be *presented* as the problem of clean air and water or conservation. This is what is meant by the "strategic use of deception." Nobody actually lies. They just withhold the whole truth.

So, suppose your position is this: "Spending class time on 'green initiatives' with children who have no background in basic science is counterproductive." Now, what's the *antithesis*, the opposite, of this position? Take a moment to think.

The facilitator will say something like this: "Kids need to be environmentally aware."

Okay. Now, toward what *synthesis* will the "facilitator" try to move the group or community—*before* any mention of a specific "green" initiative at your child's school?

Answer: The desired compromise position will probably go along the lines of: "Since energy costs are sure to rise, and 'monster-storms' are becoming more frequent, we must get children to take responsibility for human-caused climate change."

Once the provocateur finagles agreement on this "synthesis" position, then s/he can go about garnering support for anything from Cap-and-Trade posters hallways to door-to-door petition drives. *Anyone who balks will be reminded about the group consensus,* until most people "behave themselves." Nobody will want to appear "inflexible" by suggesting, for example, that barring a direct hit from an asteroid, the sun and solar flares are the primary determinants of weather, *even though most participants in the meeting may have been as skeptical as you when they walked in.*

Notice that the Left never compromises. This is another tell-tale giveaway that you're dealing with "pros." For example, you'll never hear a word about global warming being just one theory among several, even though the United Nation's Intergovernmental Panel on Climate Change backed away from this position in September 2013. If the topic is vouchers or tuition tax credits, you will never hear a word from facilitators about working with home schoolers. Consensus in the context we're discussing is a one-way street. The group will be railroaded.

How Railroading Works

3. Redefining
4. Redirecting
5. Consensus-building
6. Controlling the climate of thought
7. Marketing
8. Testing

The key to a facilitator's success, then, is controlling the environment of thought, holding on to the reins of the discussion. Your task is not to let that happen. Not at the beginning. Not an hour later. Not ever.

SECTION 4

From Provocation To Indoctrination

The right combination of marketing and provocation results in the ability to railroad opinion. Later comes indoctrination. If done properly, one <u>can</u> fool most of the people most of the time. Railroading people relies on six maneuvers, as per those discussed at the end of the previous section:

1. Redefining	4. Controlling the discussion
2. Redirecting	5. Marketing
3. Consensus-building	6. Testing

The aim is to legitimize, then institutionalize, unpopular and bogus policies before people know what's hit them. The resulting marketing package is NOT a one-size-fits-all; rather, different packages are targeted to different audiences—the business community, the intelligentsia, artists, religious leaders, schoolchildren, scientists and lawmakers.

First, let's examine "redefining terms": The public misinterprets the terms *modifying behavior, targeting attitudes,* and *outcomes.* Most of the public assumes that *behavior* means "conduct," that *attitude* means "temperament," and that *outcomes* mean "results." Not so. In the jargon of psychology, *modifying behavior* means "altering beliefs," *attitude* means "viewpoint," and *outcomes* are the "p.c."-ingrained (conditioned) gut reactions that are supposed to become second-nature.

How Students Get Duped

Schoolchildren, of course, are the easiest marks, so we should probably spend a couple of extra minutes on that. Pupils in the classroom are duped via activities, discussion groups, certain kinds of "tests," surveys, and curricular materials designed not to teach, but to deceive— usually by appealing to youngsters' egos, or by making them believe that gut reactions are real solutions without a grounding in factual knowledge. It is easy for a trained change agent standing in as a teacher to keep control of the psychological environment in a classroom using the three keys to conditioning we covered awhile ago: repetition, isolation, and labeling.

But the classroom setting is special in some respects, because raw indoctrination entails an additional spin on the usual framing of a debate.

In the classroom, you have what is known in legal terms as a *captive audience*—meaning the provocateur (teacher, principal or "guidance counselor") has *de facto* control. The kids can't simply get up and leave. But just as the media is able to dictate what Americans think about and for how long, students in today's psychology-driven classrooms are encouraged to discuss, read and engage in activities that support only a particular perspective. The difference is that an adult can always put the newspaper down or turn off the TV, but pupils can't turn off their teacher (although they sometimes tune the teacher out, but that's certainly not something you want to encourage). In any case, as soon as a pupil deviates from the preferred perspective, say in a class discussion, the topic or activity is going to be subtly changed or even ended.

This, of course, is the opposite of free expression or open discussion. But it is labeled "academic freedom" anyway.

Five Steps to Indoctrination

1. Sweep away the subject's support base—his/her intellectual and emotional life raft. Undermining parents is a favorite method of yanking the rug out from under children.
2. Bombard the subject's senses with a steady diet of conflicting, contradictory and confusing images/words (the major TV news does this, too!) in order to discourage reflection. *The result is a "vacuum" where a belief system used to be.* (We will take this one up again later.)
3. Once a vacuum has been created, leaving the subject vulnerable and impressionable (the technical term is "willing to receive stimuli"), lead the subject to the desired ideas, concepts, and

> beliefs via trained intermediaries (facilitators, "clinicians," change agents, agitators, marketing gimmicks, etc.).
> 4. Condition the subject through repeated exposure to "desired" beliefs using a wide variety of formats and activities—in other words, repeating the lies until the subject believes them.
> 5. Finally, test, survey and analyze results to ascertain whether new beliefs have been accepted. If not, repeat the whole process.

Indoctrination, like its close cousin, *brainwashing*, is a form of psychological manipulation. Indoctrination, however, goes <u>beyond</u> framing of the debate, because its purpose is not merely to <u>redirect</u> attention or <u>disrupt</u> the thought process, but *to systematically root out a person's emotional support system.* This is something that you, as an adult, must not only train *yourself* to recognize and combat; but teach your children, too. Here's how it works:

Indoctrination depends on the intermediary (say, a teacher trained as a change agent, or one of those recruits from the American Planning Association who goes out to communities and hoodwinks the locals into passing Smart Growth initiatives they'd reject on their own). The trick is that these manipulators must <u>appear</u> neutral even though the lesson, leaflets and proposals are definitely not. This is why you may sometimes notice that the new breed of teacher is called a "coach/clinician" or "mentor".

The idea is to <u>interpose</u>, *smuggle in*, as it were, certain impressions, attitudes, judgments, and conclusions into the vacuum created by stripping the belief system and "going for the gut." In this way, *viewpoints that might have been rejected by the student or focus group will appear plausible.*

Going for the Gut

A teacher's, or facilitator's, role is to *interpose* (as in interject or smuggle in), certain impressions, notions, attitudes, perceptions, and conclusions into the vacuum created by stripping away the belief system and impairing rational thought.

Helping Kids Avoid Groupthink

Teach your child how words can deceive. Explain terms like "privacy." A child can't be expected to know what's wrong with asking how much you paid for your couch, or what prescriptions are in your medicine cabinet.

It was reported by Jane S. Shaw in *National Review* magazine just how pervasive and mandatory groupthink has become on college campuses alone. To accomplish this, schools apply continuous pressure from elementary school on, causing pupils to veer liberal-left. How much they absorb depends on whom the child views as authority figures—parents, church or peers. <u>That</u> is decided in large part by which of these entities each child views as the greater threat to his ego, or which he spends the most time with.

Who's the authority figure?

The person a child relates to as an "authority figure" will be the one he perceives as being the greater threat to his feelings—or whomever he spends the most time with. If the answer is "other kids" that means the child's peers are functioning as authority figures.

Tests as Indoctrination Tools

Now, you may have noticed that testing and surveying comprise the fifth and final step to ensure a person has been successfully indoctrinated. Well, there are traditional school tests, surveys, questionnaires, polls and assessments. Then there are unexpected types of tests. For example, <u>sales figures</u> can function as a "test."

If behavioral psychologists (their curriculum is common to both advertising majors and educators) can assure the target population gets *repeated* exposure to the same "desirable" beliefs in a wide variety of formats and activities, they will probably hit a "home run." But not always.

Let's take acceptance of out-of-wedlock births, and (as we once knew it), promiscuity. These can be promoted in a variety of ways. You've probably noticed that TV plot-lines for both have been inserted ever-more-blatantly into prime time comedies, as well as in dramas such as "Grey's Anatomy," typically with a positive spin. Well, that's one way to assure changes in public perception.

Other methods include magazine ads and billboard campaigns for products that unfailingly use the term "partner," not *spouse*, not *husband*, and not *wife*.

Okay. But how do you *test* people without their knowing it to see whether these efforts are being "internalized," in the vernacular of psychologists—that is: Are the techniques *working*?

Well, you could try offering a Barbie doll knock-off called the "Gay Billy" doll or the Austin Powers doll that squawks "Are you horny, Baby?" at the child who picks it up. *The sales figures will function as a "test."* If test results are disappointing, it means resistance exists, and it is time to retool the indoctrination process; which usually entails going through the whole five-step method again. Eventually, resistance to sex-filled entertainment starts to sound "so yesterday." Once the doll is deemed funny by most parents instead of gross, then that's success. The same goes for explicit rap lyrics and video games.

The sales technique works because it bypasses the conscious, intellectual mind and shoots directly for the more vulnerable subconscious that undergirds a person's feelings and emotions. Again, it aims right for the gut.

Why Traditionalists and Constitutionalists Fail

One reason our side is getting trounced is that we don't use a multi-venue approach to "selling" our views. We have few, or no, billboards on the highway or in the subway stations. There's little effort to recruit good script writers and lobby producers; no massive effort—until, finally, the Koch Brothers (Charles and David Koch)—to buy up or take over existing media outlets. When we *do* form new outlets, we tend to label our new acquisitions "conservative" or "religious" *so that our opposition doesn't have to do it for us!*

What? You think the Big Three major mass media are saying: "Welcome to your favorite Marxist news network"?

SECTION 5

The Principles of Psych War

I alluded to Sun Tzu's book, *The Art of War*, earlier on. Now let's get down to the nitty-gritty—the principles of psych war:

Principles of Psych War

- All warfare is based on deception.
- Always let your opponent know an escape route is open so that they will go there. Show him/her that there's a road to safety so he'll think there is an alternative to losing all. Then strike.
- An enemy is conquered more easily if "appropriate conditions" are created.
- Recruit persons who are highly intelligent, but can appear stupid; who can play dumb, but are in reality strong; who are principled, but can appear passive; who are willing to be humiliated to succeed.
- Do not gobble preferred baits.
- Weary your opponents by keeping them constantly occupied. Make them rush about by offering them ostensible advantages.
- Those skilled at making an opponent move, do so by creating a situation to which he must conform—for example, by enticing him with something he is sure to take.
- Do not demand accomplishment of those who have no talent.
- Those skilled in war bring the opponent to the field of battle. They do not allow themselves to be taken or drawn there.
- Disrupt the opponent's alliances using deceptive operations so that their constituencies disperse in confusion.

- Numbers alone confer little advantage.
- Avoid the opposition when his energy is high and attack him when it is sluggish. This is control of the morale factor.
- If leaders or policies are inconsistent, morale will be low and the rank-and-file angry. Cause leaders to lose the confidence of their constituencies.

The most fundamental precept goes all the way back to Confucius: **All warfare is based on deception.**

This means <u>every</u> kind of war, not just some wars. Armed conflict or de-culturalization (which is what have been seeing for about forty-five years in this country), depends upon the ability to confuse and delude while concealing one's true nature, weaknesses, and intentions.

Always let your opponent know that an escape route is open so that they will flee. Show him/her that there is a road to safety, and so create in his/her mind that there is an alternative to losing all. Then *strike.*

Consider the allusion to an "escape route" here. Our opponents have always given us an escape route. What do we "escape" to? Legitimacy. Acceptance. What's the price? Capitulation on some issue that is more important to your adversary than the one you *think* you're talking about.

The road to "safety" is usually enticing bait on some topic of lesser importance to your adversary. Democrats allowed President George W. Bush to take credit for No Child Left Behind in 2001, even though it was the late Democratic Senator Ted Kennedy's bill, which allowed Republicans to save face with the public by claiming a victory. But once they seized this route, they were attacked from another direction.

An enemy may be conquered more easily if the appropriate conditions have been created.

"Appropriate conditions" typically involve a manufactured crisis—or exploiting a real one in order to pursue an agenda, frame the debate and control the psychological environment. As Rahm Emanuel, the Barack Obama's former Chief of Staff and later Mayor of Chicago, cynically quipped in 2009: "You never want a serious crisis to go to waste."

Proposed furloughs of Federal Aviation Administration (FAA) air-traffic controllers under "sequestration" (or *spending cuts*) in April 2013 are a perfect example of a manufactured crisis. The term "furloughing" in the context of spending meant that federal staff and contractors were not to show up for work and would not be paid over a certain number of days in a given time-period, rather than firing any of them outright. Of course, Congress never considered doing away with certain agencies altogether (especially those that have long been ineffective or unnecessary). Instead, Congress targeted agencies that were sure to impact, and annoy, the most citizens. The goal was to advance a tax-increase agenda. Senate Majority Leader Harry Reid (D-Nev.) called it "the first taste of pain," no doubt high-fiving his left-leaning colleagues as he helped create the *conditions* for an increase of the debt ceiling once again, while keeping taxes on the rise.

Repetition is an important part of "creating appropriate conditions" for an ulterior agenda. Non-stop rehashes of school shootings virtually assured there would be many more, and that they would eventually come in quick succession, not only in schools, but everywhere, such as the one on October 3, 2013, at the U.S. Capitol during the transparently manufactured crisis of a government shutdown. Over time, manufactured crises, coupled to random violence, help stoke fears of national security emergencies—creating the conditions for an imposition of martial law, curfews, bans on weapons of self-defense, mass screening for "dangerous" thoughts—all typical draconian solutions of governments-gone-awry throughout history.

Recruit persons who are highly intelligent, but can appear stupid; who are energetic, but who can appear to tire easily; who can play dumb, but are in reality strong; who are principled, but can appear passive; who are willing to be humiliated to succeed.

This axiom may appear amusing, but it is critical to success, as you will see when we get into actual battle scenarios with practice routines after the Intermediate Course.

It must be emphasized here that this axiom does not advocate "lying," as in "bearing false witness" against one's neighbor. This is *strategic deception*, which is different, like a "fake" in football. As you will see later on, this refers to the way you <u>conduct</u> yourself, not to something you say or write down *falsely* <u>about</u> somebody else.

Do not gobble preferred baits.

Our opposition throws us a bone ("bait") every once in awhile on some favorite issue, and in the process saps our energies and diverts our attention from still other topics. Too often, we take the bait without a quibble, forgetting the old adage about "picking one's battles carefully"; for example, the "bait" of gridlock.

The "Greens" are real good at selling traffic congestion, because that's a universal sore point. But then they move on to more HOV (high occupancy vehicles) lanes, which make traffic even more congested, or to taxing carbon emissions, or more environmental regulations that affect our living standards. All this wastes people's time that could be better spent on other efforts.

President Obama and his Health & Human Services Secretary, Kathleen Sebelius, did the same thing on the Health Care bill. They tried to throw the feminists a bone with free contraceptives, hoping to start a furor among the religious leaders to distract from the Left's use of the Commerce Clause to pass ObamaCare. They succeeded. Religious leaders, and other conservatives, chug-a-lugged the bait and then cried "foul."

This is not to say that the "free contraceptives" gambit wasn't a slap to many religious Christians, but at that point in time all efforts should have been directed to stopping ObamaCare completely through pressure to invoke the Commerce Clause. Once a major initiative like this is declared constitutional, it is almost impossible to remove parts of it or defund it. Prohibition is the only real exception on record.

Weary opponents by keeping them constantly occupied. Make them rush about by offering ostensible advantages.

This is another "take" on the bait-and-switch. For example, the 2013 Obama Congress pretended to be "open" to entitlement reform *if* Republicans would agree to raise taxes. Conservatives fell all over themselves to obtain favor and advantages that would never occur. Bailouts also come with promises of ostensible advantages for the nation—but, of course, typically result in additional taxes. Meanwhile, jet-setters, including many lawmakers, simply charter private planes and dodge the Transportation Security Administration, or TSA.

Environmental activists keep us so occupied arguing the rights of bugs that we've nearly forgotten about the rights of humans! So understand that your adversaries don't care, for the most part, about the unborn, maternal health, air quality, or the preservation of animal species (many of which are doing just fine, thank you). The point is to keep you occupied.

Take "medicinal marijuana": How long have we been trying to legalize marijuana–since about 1970? Well, it just kept coming up on ballot after ballot everywhere. Finally, everyone got tired of the topic, and somebody coined the term "medicinal marijuana" to take the edge off of cancer and other aimlments, which it probably did. Then marijuana stores and cafes started popping up. To borrow a line from night-time talk show mogul, Jay Leno: "Gee, who could have seen that coming??"

Race is another example: We're confronted non-stop with news centering on the problems of minorities, while gobs of taxpayer programs already are thrown at these sectors, to little effect. Yet, one rarely hears about the minorities who are making it—people like neurosurgeon Ben Carson, who in 2013 became a target of his own race for speaking out sensibly. You would think from the media that the list is limited to sports figures and Oprah. But what about standouts like singers Audra McDonald and Denyce Graves. Or columnist-author Thomas Sowell. Or talk show-columnist Armstrong Williams. Or economist-writer Walter Williams. The list spans professions ranging from entrepreneurs to business and finance. Yet these get short shrift. Overkill on racial matters is destroying Martin Luther King, Jr.'s "dream" of a colorblind society.

Those skilled at making an opponent move do so by creating a situation to which s/he must conform—for example, by enticing him with something he is sure to take.

By way of example, in the 1980s the US Department of Education came up with a means of supposedly jump-starting competitive, academic test scores called The Nation's Report Card—something folks were sure to accept. Of course, test scores continued declining. Under the Obama administration, we have Common Core of Standards, which bring new meaning to federal control and data-mining. So, by creating conditions in which academic scores are *sure to fall* and then *reporting dismal results annually*, government assures an endless need for more taxpayer funding!

Don't demand accomplishment of those who have no talent.

This sounds laughable and obvious, but it isn't. For example, in congressional offices most staff advisors for education—regardless of party affiliation—have no expertise in that field or, for that matter, any knowledge concerning the major players and vested interests in schools. Worse, the position tends to be viewed as a stepping-stone for political science majors barely out of college toward something more exciting. Many of these staffers are the sons or daughters of important "somebodies" in government, and that's how they break into these jobs. But the information that passes through these young staffers' hands on education is critical to good policymaking. Here's a true story about two congressional staffers at one of the NASA centers. The topic was the need for new and improved weather satellites. Representatives of the National Oceanic and Atmospheric Administration (NOAA) made the presentation.

In the midst of the lecture, a youngish staffer leaned toward his colleague and was overheard to say: "I don't see why we need all these satellites when I can just download the weather any time I want to my cell phone." *And his colleague nodded in agreement!*

Chalk that one up to the "Classic Blooper" Department!

Here were *two* US college graduates who apparently had never considered where, exactly, their vaunted weather downloads originated. They'd probably learned all about recycling and man-made global-warming "destroying the planet." Imagine how these staffers will advise their boss in Congress on energy and "sustainable development" issues!

Only the most experienced and talented persons should hold such advisory-research positions, and they should be well-paid so that it's clear that a low-profile position in research is nevertheless highly valued.

Those skilled in war bring the opponent to the field of battle. They do not allow themselves to be drawn or taken there.

How is it that we always wind up debating issues on our adversary's turf? When we go to meetings, it is at a time and place of ***their*** choosing, not ours. For example, when we debate in a public forum, it's frequently the promise of mainstream network coverage that gets us there—and guess whose agenda gets the positive coverage? Face time with the media is the bait, and we take it. Now, suppose we invited our adversaries—say, Al Gore—to debate "climate change," on <u>our</u> turf, for example to a face-off at the conservative Heritage Foundation? What do you think would happen? He'd laugh and blow us off.

This harkens back to the **Alinsky Method**—Saul Alinsky's *Rules for Radicals* again. Among his "rules" was this: "There can be no conversation between the organizer and his opponents. The latter must be depicted as being evil." He wrote further: "You don't communicate with anyone purely on the rational facts or ethics of an issue." Nothing wishy-washy about that statement.

Columnist Jack Kerwick explains that Alinsky's bottom line consisted of three tenets: to polarize the debate, to demonize anyone who stands in the way, and avoid giving opponents a human face. That means, our leftists adversaries are not going to debate our experts, no matter how many advanced degrees they may have, and especially not on our turf, because to do so would provide us public credibility. That's why all those ads in conservative periodicals (online and print) asking—indeed daring—Al Gore or somebody on his side to debate experts like Lord Christopher Monckton, former adviser to the late Prime Minister Margaret Thatcher, "ain't gonna happen."

Disrupt the opponent's alliances using deceptive operations . . . so that their constituencies disperse in confusion.

Notice how our once-firm religious alliances, for example—the ones that supported conservatives during, and prior to, the Reagan years—have "dispersed in confusion," over issues like same-sex "marriage," "sustainable development," and the "Fiscal Cliff." That's why we never get anywhere, because we have no agreed-upon strategy. Our constituencies "see" that and withhold their further support.

Numbers *alone* confer little advantage.

Numbers of people marching around don't make much difference. Numbers of people with a mission and a plan do. Jesus had had only twelve disciples, but they changed the world.

Avoid the opposition when his energy is high and attack him when it is sluggish to control the morale factor.

That one is fairly obvious.

When leaders or policies are inconsistent, morale will be low and the rank-and-file angry. When factions . . . gather and whisper, leaders have lost the confidence of constituents.

Inconsistency in policymaking rules the day. We *have* laws—for example, obscenity laws—that even the Justice Department doesn't bother enforcing, to the detriment of children. Yet, political correctness on *zero-tolerance* policies results in asinine repercussions like the kid disciplined as a "Pop-Tart® Terrorist."

No wonder morale among good, stable people is low. The rank-and-file are angry, but obviously not angry enough. America's backbone of citizens has lost confidence in its leaders.

Congress itself has never been held in such low esteem—to the point where voting records show most citizens to be downright apathetic.

INTERMEDIATE COURSE—LOOSE LOGIC

Introduction

The way in which the mind goes about drawing conclusions is based upon habitual patterns of logic. Some mental habits result in fallacious logic—that is, sloppy or "loose" reasoning.

Thought disruption can result in the inability to sustain a line of reasoning from beginning to conclusion. Sometimes the cause is interruptions, noise and other distractions. Take television: This cultural phenomenon has contributed to the inability to hold a train of thought or even to grasp context. Today's ear-splitting, special-effects-driven commercials every six minutes make it difficult to follow more than a cartoonish plot line. The Left has taken advantage of that. TV has become more an addiction than entertainment. News tends to be "info-tainment," not real *reportage* or *journalism*.

Another example of distraction is the non-stop interruptions built into a typical school day. These have impaired children's ability to concentrate and are frequently mistaken for a nonexistent malady popularly called Attention Deficit Disorder (ADD). The "deficit" lies in the disturbances in teaching and learning created by schools—disturbances that once were not allowed. ADHD, or Attention Deficit Hyperactivity Disorder, is often an extension of ADD: The child becomes disruptive because his energy has to go somewhere. He cannot follow the lesson and his classroom is already chaotic. What so-called child experts point to as "hyperactive," is in reality pent-up frustration coupled to a long-term lack of structure and discipline.

Most young children crave a predictable world, some sort of order and routine they can count on day-to-day, or they become fussy and irritable. Most parents used to know this intuitively; no one had to tell them. It is the rare child who thrives in a predominantly non-structured environment; most can only take it for so long—as in what we used to call "recess." (Some schools are stupidly phasing out recess in order to, supposedly, augment instruction time.) But child psychologists came along in the 1950s and told parents and teachers all that was mistaken. By the 1970s, the "Free to Be" movement was in full swing. We've been paying for it with swelling populations in detention centers, jails and prisons ever since.

Which brings us back to compromised "mental habits" which exacerbate the tendency toward fallacies of logic. A fallacy can be as simple as a deceptive maneuver intended to bolster an argument for which there is insufficient evidence. Sometimes we deceive ourselves, but whether the fallacy was committed accidentally or on purpose is incidental.

Other times our reasoning capabilities are simply hijacked. Law students, for example, learn how to psychologically "hijack" a jury and even falsely augment a case by bringing up non-germane issues. The opposing attorney is supposed to catch this sort of thing and say "Objection" on the grounds of "relevance." But sometimes the distraction is so smooth that it gets a pass, and the judge is helpless to do anything about it. Even if a judge sustains the objection called by the opposing attorney, a jury, in reality, cannot "disregard" something that has been planted in their mind—and neither can you.

Prospective facilitators, provocateurs and change-agents get some of the same psychology training as attorneys, then are sent out to neighborhoods and schools: Among the more disconcerting mental-hijacking techniques are:

- misquoting or incompletely quoting
- dismissing alternatives
- changing the subject or from it
- exaggerating facts
- insulting opponents

These work because lay audiences since the 1940s have not been required to take a course called "logic" in high school. So they are not expected to be able to pick up on faulty reasoning.

A classic, case highlighting at least three of the above techniques occurred in the much-publicized case against George Zimmerman, the Neighborhood Watch volunteer who shot and killed young Trayvon Martin. The government's (and the lapdog media's) handling of this case combined distraction, exaggeration and change of subject in a particularly deceptive and destructive way.

Everyone was led to believe that the issues in this case related to stereotyping and race, irrespective of the fact that the defendant, Zimmerman, is basically a white Hispanic.

The facts are more disquieting. A mountain of evidence suggests that government couldn't have cared less about any racial implications— or, for that matter, about Trayvon Martin and George Zimmerman! The case was not even about murder. What they *did* care about was Neighborhood Watch programs. Race was merely a convenient means of discrediting "self-styled" security schemes, which the Justice Department has long since gone on record as despising, complete with warnings to employees.

Think about it—especially in light of terrorism and the increasingly brazen affronts against citizens by the likes of the TSA. If a country has hundreds of thousands of Neighborhood Watch programs scattered about, and the elected volunteers are armed, what, in effect, do you have? You have a supposed breeding ground for an armed militia.

How easy is it going to be for a subsequent administration to declare martial law and roll tanks down Main Street with potential militias at the ready all over the place?

Here's a bet for you: How much less enthusiasm has already been generated, and how many fewer average folks have volunteered, for Neighborhood Watch programs than, say, in 2012? How many, in light of all the hype surrounding this case, are going to put their reputations, lives and finances on the line if one error in judgment justified or not, is going to bring a person down?

Here is an overview of *fallacies of logic*, all aimed at bolstering an argument, either accidentally or deliberately.

Common Fallacies

- oversimplifications
- smears
- false hypotheses and analogies
- hasty generalizations
- straw-man arguments
- irrelevancies
- false appeals
  - to fear
  - to expertise
  - to popularity
  - to common practice

Throw in distractions, which we already discussed, and deviations such as misaligned (or "out-of-sync") cause-effect gaffes, circular reasoning, lack of qualifier words, and ill-defined terms, and your task becomes even harder.

Related Reasoning Mis-Fires

- Misaligned cause-effect
- Circular reasoning
- Dubious evidence
- Contradictory arguments
- Lack of qualifier terms
- Ill-defined terms

Let's start with *oversimplifications* and *smears*.

SECTION 1

The Oversimplification

Oversimplification is one of the most-used tricks in the business. The fallacy stems from a normal desire to *impose orderliness on complex facts*. **Slogans** are typical of oversimplification: "Make love, not war!" "Go Green!" "Safe Sex." "Legalize Love." That sort of thing. These oversimplify issues and promote pseudo-solutions. Here's a *set* of catch-phrases used in the field of education. Together, these comprise a sloganized *bundle*.

- "All children can learn."
- "Success breeds success."
- "Schools must level the playing field."

These expressions are easy to remember, contain only a few words— and vastly oversimplify the issue of learning. In responding to "all children can learn," you can innocently ask: "Are you saying that all people have identical abilities? That they can all learn the same things, sooner or later?"

In response to "success breeds success," you can ask: "How about apathy? Can success breed apathy?"

In response to the third—"Schools must level the playing field"—you might ask: "Does emphasis on leveling the playing field early on create false expectations and damage the incentive of the best and brightest?"

Think back to the Principles of Psych-War—which ones are invoked in these comeback questions?

Answers:

- <u>Frame the debate</u> and create the "appropriate conditions" for battle.
- Prepare the groundwork for <u>controlling the psychological environment</u>.
- Plant <u>seeds of dissent</u> to help bolster weaker supporters.

Posing counter-arguments in the form of questions tends to plant seeds of doubt among fence-sitters. But, if you have to do all asking yourself, you can also be easily isolated. So, it's helpful to go in with one or more supporters who can be counted upon to chime in their agreement. Be sure to sit at <u>different places</u> in the room so that support doesn't appear choreographed.

SECTION 2

The Smear

The smear (or masked insults) is a popular technique. The best way to approach a smear is to treat it as a distraction, which also functions as an alienation strategy.

If you are dealing with a smear—or even an implied smear—you absolutely must keep track of the <u>specific</u> topic you're on to avoid being trapped into debating a related or different one.

Here are some lead-in lines that a facilitator, or even an agitator seated beside you, might say:

> **"Even a child would see [that seat-time in a classroom doesn't equate to proficiency in subject matter.]"**

It doesn't matter, by the way, what topic you put in the brackets. It's the part <u>before</u> the brackets that comprises the red flag. The topic, in this case, is important, but secondary.

In the example here, you have been called childish. The implication is that you are naïve and inexperienced. An appropriate response might be:

> *"Well, perhaps children don't have the maturity to understand that indulging in frantic activity doesn't necessarily mean proficiency."*

Then address the <u>subject</u>, without pausing, like this:

> *"I will concede that time sitting at a desk frequently has translated to social promotion, and endless repetition without any remedial help. But I do **not** agree that replacing so-called "seat time," or teacher instruction, equates to measurable results. . . ."*

The thing you must avoid is contradicting your opponent's smear of "childish." Doing so will only serve to divert your audience. Make your point instead.

Another approach is to use humor. For example, suppose a facilitator or an agitator says to you:

> *"Even a right-wing Fundamentalist would admit [that children need to learn to protect themselves against sexually transmitted diseases.]"*

You should respond with something like this:

> *"Yeah, I know our friend here just called me a wacko right-wing Bible-thumper. She would probably have called Mother Theresa a cultist. Before we get too carried away with all this stereotyping, let's get back to the subject at hand which, I believe, was . . . ."*

And then continue. **Under no circumstances, even if you're an atheist, should you deny the charge** your attacker has made: right-wing Fundamentalist. Why?

Answer: Because you don't want to come from a <u>defensive</u> position. If you do, you'll <u>never</u> be permitted to discuss the real issue, which is appropriate health curriculum. All your time, and that of other group members, will be taken up arguing religion and/or religious bias. The term "right-wing Fundamentalist" is a provocation, pure and simple. Any yes, go ahead and throw the word "stereotyping" back, because that's a slogan favored by leftists and will win over fence-setters in the group to <u>your</u> side.

Here again are some other variations on a smear:

> *"Even **you** will admit [that HIV infection is a problem.]"*

This lead-in line (even **you**) is an <u>implied</u> smear. The purpose is to intimidate you, and put you on the defensive. This may happen if you are deemed a genuine treat to what the facilitator is trying to "sell" the group. S/he needs to keep you in a "reactive" mode.

The next version is a little tougher:

> *"A person who really wanted to improve education [would agree that all children need a chance to succeed.]"*

Now, why is that a smear?

To the uninitiated, the comment sounds reasonable. Again, the smear is by <u>implication</u>. Inasmuch as you have not been labeled <u>outright</u>, you run the danger of looking stupid if you jump to the bait and say something like: "I do <u>so</u> care about improving education" or "about the environment" or whatever. A professional agitator's comeback to such a defensive remark would be: "Miss Smith, I don't recall having said *you* didn't care about improving education."

Another **poor response** to this "come-on" is a question like: "What kind of person would *not* want to improve education?"

Normally a pithy question like this would put your attacker on the spot. But not this time. S/he will simply say something such as: *"a controlling person, someone like you."* You don't want to give the attacker a forum. Best to defuse the whole *"chance to succeed"* remark, with something like this:

You, Version 1: *"That makes sense. The problem is deciding what form that 'chance to succeed' should take."*

Or, you could try a more cheeky response:

You, Version 2: *"Okay. And your point is?"*

And say it in a bored, neutral tone of voice.

Now, you may wonder: Why should I play nice with this jerk? Because, by implication, you are also denying that *you* are "the person" the jerk is referring to. You are defusing a hostile situation and bought yourself and your group time. The provocateur now has to change tactics or "hang himself," so to speak. S/he has to change the subject entirely, or accuse you then and there of being against educational reform, *which would make the provocateur look worse than you.*

SECTION 3

The Hasty Generalization

Suppose a facilitator were to say something like this:

As you know, kids are maturing faster these days. This means homosexuality must be part of our elementary health curriculum.

What's wrong with this logic?

This facilitator makes a typical mistake, and don't get distracted by the issue. Examine the next two comments for their similarities to the facilitator's statement. Which one is true, the first, the second, or both?

- **"People live longer today."**
- **"People have longer life spans today."**

Answer: Only the first one is true. The human life <u>span</u> has not changed in thousands of years. Copious records attest to life spans as long as ninety to a little over one hundred, dating from the time of Confucius. What *has* changed is that, proportionally, <u>more people</u> are living to into their eighties and nineties, thanks to medical technology. In countries without such technology, fewer people live that long. But to say that suddenly the world is producing two-hundred-year-old people is without basis. The facilitator's comment that youngsters are maturing earlier is similarly flawed. It's a *hasty generalization*.

Here's a comeback you can use for the facilitator's flawed argument—made to bolster support for grade-school homosexuality curricula:

You: Are children really more mature today? That's a pretty sweeping generalization: Just because youngsters can draw more spectacular pornographic pictures on their desks, or because they know more four-letter words than we did, hardly makes them "mature." Girls in the Middle East, Latin America, and Asia typically have started menstruating at younger ages than white Anglos, and this is now changing due to inter-marriage. But secondary sex characteristics are purely physical and do *not* translate to maturity of judgment. People used to be aware of that, by being careful, for example, that young girls were chaperoned. But by *emancipating children*, we now are deluged with reports about American schoolgirls suffering gang rapes and vicious bullying. I challenge you to come up with any evidence that American pupils, or kids anywhere, for that matter, are demonstrating emotional maturity earlier.

Notice that you haven't mentioned homosexuality or gay curriculum. You have merely attacked the facilitator's flawed basis of argument. That gives you much more leverage, because you have deftly planted seeds of doubt concerning health curricula in general—which, as we know, focuses very little on general physiology and systems of the body, such as the digestive, respiratory, nervous, and circulatory systems.

SECTION 4

The False Hypothesis

A hypothesis is an unproven theory, conjecture, assumption, or perhaps an educated guess. But however "educated" a theory or assumption may be, it cannot be used to draw a conclusion unless something credible exists to support it.

Frequently, a theory or assumption contains a **kernel** of truth, but these kernels often carry major discrepancies. They don't support the conclusion drawn from them. If two theories, or "educated guesses," are paired with each other—"*this* plus *that* means such-and-such"—it's sometimes hard to interrupt and say, "Wait a minute, the two things you just said don't go together."

Complicating Factors in Logic

The major discrepancies that grow from a *false hypothesis* may include

- false assumptions
- misaligned cause-effect (are out-of-sync, lacking in correlation, or rely on coincidental events)
- failure to "qualify" the argument
- dubious evidence
- contradictory data

Most items here are fairly self-explanatory. All are easily avoided. But you can nail your opponent on them—right away, if you're quick, or when your adversary comes up for air. That provides you an opportunity to bust up his, or her, argument.

Unfortunately, not all such mistakes are easy to spot.

"Therefores" and "Givens"

Think of <u>every</u> false hypothesis as a "therefore"-type argument. Picture it as one two diagrams:

Reasoning (i.e., supportive evidence)   Hypothesis (theory or "given") → conclusion

Or:

Alternative Reasoning (+ supportive evidence)   Cause → effect

Every theory is based on one or more assumptions, or "givens." As in geometry, if the assumption—that is, the "given"—is false, off the subject, biased, or exaggerated, then the conclusion will suffer accordingly. Sometimes a speaker places his assumption at the beginning; other times at the end, but these are normal <u>speech</u> <u>patterns</u>.

Professional manipulators, as well as average people, may launch their argument with mistaken, or even deliberately misleading statements that are in reality their own opinions, perceptions, or those "educated guesses" we talked about earlier. They dive right into their conclusion (the "therefore" or "consequently" part), <u>before</u> anyone can challenge them. If you are quick, and you can equate it with one of those word problems you used to get in math class, you may be able to stop your opponent cold, particularly if he, or she, puts the "given/ assumption" first. If the assumption is placed at the end (that is, <u>after</u> the "therefore"), or if it just takes you a minute to recognize that what you're hearing is a "therefore" diagram based on a "false hypothesis," then it is best let your opponent "hang himself." Let him finish.

The hardest task for you is to avoid getting sidetracked by distractions and irrelevancies. As with those pesky word problems you faced in your math classes, you must ignore what you don't need, and keep your attention fixed on the "givens" (i.e., the assumptions or hypotheses). Repeat over and over to yourself your opponent's wording if you have to, so as to tune out the irrelevant stuff. Having identified a false assumption, forget for the time being about whether the rest of your opponent's reasoning is poor, or whether it contains inconsistencies. As soon as your opponent "comes up for air," *raise your hand and nail him on that wrong assumption, or hypothesis, and stay ahead of the game.* This assures you control of the debate.

Variation 1: "Cause-Effect" Out of Sync

Sometimes the "effect" simply does not logically follow the "cause." This falls into the category of a *misaligned* ("out-of-sync") *cause-effect* argument. The key to countering this variation is to come up with a *different*, but <u>reasonable</u>, alternative. Suppose a community organizer says this:

"We've all noticed an uptick in "monster storms" worldwide, so any case against climate change is closed. We must institute new regulations if we expect to save the planet."

Where is the "effect" in the above statement?

Answer: *The "effect" is new regulations for "climate change."* This is a non-negotiable position, placed at the end of the sentence.

What, then, is the "cause," the hypothesis and assumption?

The cause is "monster storms"—a term which, by the way, also serves in this case as a great slogan. But this "in-person assister," or organizer, inadvertently gives away the game with the words "we've all noticed." Think back to the techniques of psych-war. Why are these three words a giveaway?

Answer: An attempt to create a "we" mentality: We're all in this together, right? So, how are you going to deflect this one?

You attack your opponent's "given" hypothesis—climate change and the accompanying slogan, *monster storms.* Hundreds of scientists have concluded that temperatures haven't changed **overall** since 1800, when there were no SUVs, much less heating or air conditioning. And monster storms have been a fact of life forever—monsoon seasons in India and Southeast Asia, centuries of typhoons in the western and northeast Pacific regions, routine blizzards and temperatures of −50° in Minnesota. Throughout recorded history, some regions experience a spate of extreme weather over several years before returning to the usual ups and downs for their geographical locations. To suggest that "monster storms" are a new phenomenon falsely exaggerates the facts. Climate activists could not change overall weather variations and patterns—amounts of rainfall, cold and heat—if they wanted to.

Variation 2: Failure to "Qualify" an Argument

Sometimes an argument suffers simply from a lack of <u>qualifier</u> terms to allow for exceptions and the occasional mistake. Examples of such terms include *"significant numbers of"* and *"seems to be."* Words like *"always"* and *"never"* don't provide you any leeway. Give yourself an "out" in case you are mistaken; in case data is miscalculated; in case, under pressure, you use one person's name when you mean someone else. You don't want to give up the reins of an entire debate when a simple qualifier will do. You don't want to get caught up in a contest, for instance, over <u>precisely</u> how many scientists said this or that, because doing so would take you to a *de*fensive position. If asked, you can always offer to exchange e-mail addresses or phone numbers with a challenger so you can provide an exact answer to small particulars later. Then move on. Using qualifier words, and/or promising to get back with specifics later, tends to shut down hostile opponents who are determined to stick to their agenda regardless of how many facts you provide.

Here's a quick test for you right now. What term did I just use in the last sentence that is a "qualifier"?

Answer: "tends to."

Here are two additional examples of misaligned arguments which suffer only for lack of qualifiers. Which is more accurate?

1. Crime is caused by low self-esteem.
2. Low self-esteem contributes to delinquency.

The answer is that both statements contain a kernel of truth. But the second statement is more accurate, because of the qualifier term *"contributes to."*

But looking only at option #*1* above, it's fair to ask how many delinquents have <u>high</u> self-esteem—too high, in fact. Is there *another reasonable cause* of crime? Yes: idleness, lack of adult guidance and supervision, lack of religious/moral training, fatherless children, etc. The first statement (#*1*), then—"crime is caused by low self-esteem"— can either be debunked outright, or calls for a qualifier term: "Crime <u>can</u> *be* caused by low self-esteem."

While the second statement already contains a qualifier, it is still not a completely accurate. Why?

Because the statement is not true *across the board*. Nevertheless, you will find statement #2 used to bolster support for "busing," racial quotas, same-sex dates for prom night, women in front-line combat—all of which have <u>roots</u> in self-esteem. That does not mean, however, that low self-esteem always contributes to crime. Sometimes it is actually a spur to do better, try harder, make oneself a stand-out in a chosen field. As the sentence stands, even the qualifier "contributes to" *implies* that it always contributes to crime. So, you must be very careful with these kinds of comments—a problem of news journalism.

So here's a good response to comments 1 and 2:

Good Comeback:
"Perhaps self-esteem is a factor in *some* children. But other likely causes are . . . ."

Then, list some alternatives: lax discipline, fatherless children, etc. This way, you avoid a confrontation, and "own" the debate. Don't play up the self-esteem issue at all; the person who made the original remark should be forced to put more credible causes of delinquency on the table for discussion, or else "fold."

Biasing an Argument

In April 2013, a radio newscast came out with a lead story that (inadvertently?) left out a pertinent fact. Like the two congressional staffers (see "Principles of Psych-War") who didn't seem to know where the "apps" on their weather downloads originated, the result was another "classic blooper."

The good news, according to the report, was that smoking was way down in the United States from what it was in the 1960s–1990s.

Then, the commentators moved quickly from this good news to the topic of obesity, which was alleged to have reached "epidemic" proportions. Unless a person was *really* paying attention to the broadcast, they would have missed a long-unmentioned fact: the reason why so many Americans either took up, or kept on, smoking even after the habit was proved dangerous. Prior to the 1980s, common wisdom had it that smoking kept one *thinner*. And indeed, that *is* frequently a side-effect. Thousands of people put on twenty or thirty pounds once they quit smoking.

Undoubtedly a balanced diet and fewer calories are positive actions, and smoking is dangerous to health for a variety of reasons (among them, a trigger for lung or throat cancer, emphysema, etc.). But failure to mention *why* so many people once smoked—to stay thin and avoid giving up ice cream and other heavy foods—compromises both the anti-obesity and the anti-smoking campaigns. That means the over-45 crowd is apt to *subconsciously tune out* the healthy diet messages. They still perceive a positive link between thinness and smoking.

So here again, the condition called *cognitive dissonance*, noted toward the beginning of this course, has kicked in: Two irreconcilable "authorities" are waging war in the people's memory banks. Since many folks cannot resolve the conflicting evocations, they tune *both* "health" messages out. What happens is that the emotional mind tells the intellectual "think for yourself" mind to kindly just shut up.

There is more on this phenomenon in the Advanced Course.

SECTION 5

The False Analogy

You are probably familiar with the *false analogy*, as per the old saying "comparing apples with oranges." But as with the anti-smoking/healthy eating message, it can get more complicated than you think. Take, for example, the following situation:

> A local housing authority is placing a drug-abuse rehabilitation center ("halfway house") in an upper-middle-class suburb. Angry residents converge upon the town council in force, waving a report saying property values are already depressed by 30 percent. In a meeting, a housing authority calls this report invalid, stating that there is, in fact, no drop in individual house prices because real estate agents say houses are selling like hot cakes, even better than last year and three years before that.

What's going wrong here? [**Think before continuing.**]

Answer: The housing authority has changed the subject and produced a false analogy. The subject was changed to **pace of sales**, when in fact residents were complaining about **depressed property values**. Indeed, the lower property values (or, house prices) could be the *reason* for brisk sales! People that once could not *afford* a house in this neighborhood could now do so. So, while both parties are discussing houses, the housing authority is using an argument not related to the residents' complaints.

To complicate this scenario further, residents were probably intimidated by the prospect of appearing politically incorrect to representatives of the housing authority, which smacks of an "appeal to fear." What residents more than likely *wanted* to say was that they didn't like what they perceived as "a criminal element" or "drug menace" near their homes. So, they masked their real source of angst out of fear of appearing "intolerant." This created a perfect storm for the town council to move along with the plan, solving nothing and misreading the real subject.

Moreover, in a meeting of "concerned citizens" like this, if, while listening, *you get the nagging feeling that something is out-of-whack, something probably is.*

Another instance of a *false analogy* can be found in a manual put out in the 1990s by a state arm of the NEA, "What's Left After the Right," which I also refer to in the Advanced Course. It implies that primarily Christians advocate the phonics method of teaching reading and spelling (probably because of the old McGuffey Readers which today's parents may not even remember). Thus are Christians targeted for criticizing the more "progressive" methodology, which endorses a "sight," or "whole language" approach to teaching children to read and spell.

Sight and *whole language* methods stress <u>context</u> <u>clues</u>, as well as the overall "look" of a word. Phonics stresses understanding a "code"—that is, the <u>sounds</u> which various blends of letters tend to stand for—so that young pupils get into the habit of transferring these letter combinations from one text to another. Only about 15 percent of the language is non-phonetic, so phonics vastly <u>de</u>creases the number of words students have to actually memorize in order to read or spell.

Unfortunately, this entire debate is lost when phonics is falsely identified with Christians. The knee-jerk reaction is to dismiss phonics as religiously based. Leftists are the ones who are intolerant of any teaching method except the so-called "progressive," or trendy, fads, and they have "prepped" the public, especially teachers, to view anything Christian as biased. So, equating religion with a teaching method creates a particularly harmful *false analogy* because no one can argue the real issue.

SECTION 6

The Irrelevancy

Many distorted arguments are the result of irrelevancies being inserted into the mix, advertently and inadvertently. This causes people to "go off on tangents," usually because they have become emotional. The person may start out well, but then loses his frame of reference, changes the subject, and ruins his argument with irrelevant chatter.

What happens is, various arguers throw in their two cents—maybe even the moderator of the discussion—and everyone proceeds to interrupt each other. The result becomes more about the other person's overall politics than about the subject at hand. The debate drifts off so nobody can follow it, onto tangential topics that are not key to the original question being debated.

This scenario was highly noticeable in the 2012 presidential and vice-presidential televised debates. Go on the Internet and find videos of these debates, then examine these at length for *irrelevant tangents*. Ask yourself: Can I follow this? Did anyone answer the question here?

SECTION 7

The Straw-Man Argument

A *straw-man argument is one in which a position is attacked when there is no one there to defend it.* A non-existing or non-present entity is attacked, so there is little chance of being proved wrong. Take the following exchange:

Greg: What do you make of those eight thousand people who marched against ObamaCare?

Patty: I think they're a bunch of nuts who have enough money to finance everything themselves.

Greg: How so?

Patty: Average people should have a say in how health care is provided. Throwing out the government just because you don't like your insurance company is crazy.

Greg: Well, I don't think they should throw out the government, either.

Greg just suffered a "brain freeze." He wound up flustered and responded instead to a provocation from Patty, whether she intended it or not. Patty's provocative remark was actually an understated straw-man argument. Whether she was right or not, no one from the government, including (presumably) the protesters, was there to back up ObamaCare or any other nationalized health care program. In fact, most of them probably were not rich, either, because that is not the type of person who typically protests in large groups. (Donald Trump marching around with a sign? Probably not.) So, one can safely assume other reasons. Patty actually left herself open to challenge. But she didn't get one from Greg. Neither Patty nor Greg had an inkling of how to debate issues.

Did all of the protesters want to subsidize their own health care, 100 percent of the time, including that of their elderly, extended families—forever? Today, probably not. Only billionaires can really afford to do that and still keep their homes. And billionaires are not marching with signs.

So, regardless of your opinion on government-subsidized health care, on Mr. Obama, or even insurance companies, Greg's best bet would have been to handle this as a straw-man argument. He should have responded with something like this:

COMEBACK:
"You know, I haven't actually *heard* the pros and cons on this. Before I decide, I'd like to hear from doctors, insurance heads and persons *not vested in* the protest."

Most of us are simply not well enough versed in the tricks of the rhetorical trade to pick up on such subtleties. This makes it easy for professional manipulators—usually agitators in this case—to aggressively recruit college students and wannabe activists to advocate, demonstrate and participate in petition drives on subjects that require some sort of expertise and experience.

SECTION 8

Circular Reasoning

The circular argument (sometimes known as "begging the question") is tricky. It all depends upon those "givens" we discussed in the section on cause-and-effect. If the "given," or assumption, is true, you may be able to pull it off. But when you are expected to cite evidence to justify your thesis, or "given," it is difficult to respond unless you have something more than your original opinion. In other words, the hypothesis and the conclusion should not be identical. Take, for example, the following exchange:

Parent: "These curriculums on homosexuality are wrong, destroy morals, undercut parental teachings, and have no place in the public schools."

Principal: "Why do you say that?"

Parent: "Because it runs counter to the Bible."

Principal: "That's a pretty narrow view. What makes the Bible an authority on curriculum?"

Parent: "Because the Bible is the inspired word of God and it specifically condemns homosexuality, that's why."

The parent in this exchange should have realized as soon as the principal asked "what makes the Bible an authority on curriculum" that he was not going to buy her argument. So, her position came across as "circular reasoning." This parent should have immediately switched gears and risked a change of subject ("re-direction") to justify her position. For example, the parent could have deftly woven in medical considerations:

Parent: "Because religious and ethical systems for thousands of years of civilization have taught that homosexuality demeans the human spirit, is physically harmful, and is not in the best interests of society. Nearly all physicians agree on that."

But, suppose the principal is a quick study and responds like this:

Principal: "Well, there's a lot of debate today on all of that."

In that case, an alert parent should respond with this "gotcha":

Parent: "Exactly. That's why young children should not be getting curriculum that bolsters only one view. In fact, given the nature of the debate, homosexuality is _not_ an inappropriate topic for children, who have _no clinical background in medicine._"

SECTION 9

The Appeals

A universally popular tactic of most debaters is *the appeal*—appeals to fear, to expertise, to popularity, to common practice. Appeals are used by the good guys and the bad guys with equal gusto because appeals are based on the *power of suggestion*. Fortunately, most appeals are fairly easy to spot—once you know what to look for—and you can nail your opponent on them.

An excellent example of the first, *appeal to fear*, is found in handout literature that characterizes detractors and critics as conservative, religious Right, and extremist. Recall that this was one reason that housing authority representatives misread their audience under the section on false analogies. Gullible folks are to assume, of course, that nobody <u>except</u> conservatives and religious people ever complain. So, the implied "fear" in this case is an implied, stigmatizing label, "fanatic."

Appeals to popularity (also known as *"herd approval"*) are rooted in the inclination to conform and respond to the crowd. Remember Marx's Theory of Alienation, from the beginning of this course?

When you hear the phrases "everyone knows. . .", "it's common knowledge that. . .", or "we are all aware of. . .," it signals that an *appeal to popularity* and/or an *appeal to fear* will follow. Most people do not want to be the only person who "doesn't know" something or "isn't aware" of something. We fear appearing ignorant.

The appeal can a bit more elusive, however.

For example, PBS's Nightly Business Report (NBR) aired a segment March 21, 2013, explaining how large companies like the CVS drug chain are forcing so-called "wellness programs" on their employees, including a demand that workers disclose their private medical information, called "health benchmarks," plus information about health-related "*behaviors*," such as smoking (but apparently *not* risky sexual conduct).

The alternative to giving up your privacy, apparently, was to pay a $600 fine for increased health insurance premiums!

This particular wellness policy is clearly "data-driven"—meaning that the so-called <u>privacy</u> notice you have to sign every time you visit a new doctor or pick up a prescription, the Health Insurance Portability and Accountability Act (HIPAA), is a sham.

Confused yet?

There has long been a capability to cross-match and share information—whether in the name of making people healthier and "saving" on overall health-care costs, or something else. The CVS policy raised the hackles of Dr. Deborah C. Peel, patient privacy rights champion; she was interviewed for her thoughts on the matter by NBR. Dr. Peel alleged that millions of patients avoid cancer screenings and other tests out of fear of privacy violations, which made the CVS policy highly controversial. However, she was careful to praise Big Company investments in "wellness" and to encourage behaviors commonly associated with good health. (She knew she was walking a fine "p.c." line.)

So, NBR quizzed an average citizen on the issue. The interviewed woman contended that the CVS mandate was okay with her because—*get this!*—she "had nothing to hide."

Think about that: Nothing To Hide. The CVS policy in question actually contains <u>two</u> subjects: privacy and wellness. Which of these was this "average citizen" responding to?

The answer is both—one intentionally; the other, not so much.

One first subject, "wellness," functions today as a craze, on a par with the fitness trend of the 1980s and later, the vegetarian diet. For this reason, it is an oblique appeal to popularity, because all trends and fads *derive their legitimacy* from popularity.

This is *not* to say that exercise is goofy or that vegetarianism is a mistake. It's a choice, and maybe a good one for many people. But the *hype* and *pressure* applied to exercise, vegetarianism and, now, wellness, is an inducement **to buy something**, to sign up for something (usually expensive)—say, a health club, organic foods, and an abundance of feel-good-quick "miracle" vitamins and remedies, and "it does everything" exercise equipment—some of which are legitimate and even work. Others, of course, are scams. Either way, all these fads fall under a popularity label.

For the many individuals at risk for other medical problems, such as osteoporosis, food or drug intolerances and multiple allergic reactions, popular fads can be dicey.

For example, pressure to exercise endlessly, for the sake of seeming "with it," may spell a person's doom. A Maryland woman suffering from undiagnosed, poorly aligned, weak joints, forced herself to jog up the escalators every evening from the subway as part of a self-imposed adjunct exercise regimen. She was only in her thirties, but wound up with multiple hairline fractures in both kneecaps.

A school principal in Texas jogged every evening—and dropped dead on the pavement at age forty-three from a heart attack.

Organic fruits and vegetables are not necessarily "cleaner" than their non-organic counterparts as popularly believed. Some may even be grown in contaminated "natural" fertilizers. Nevertheless, they are billed as "healthier," and typically are more expensive.

All this gives new meaning to the term "overkill."

So, if you thought that the "average" citizen interviewed by NBR who had "nothing to hide" was a proud response to concerns about "privacy," it was probably more an appeal to fear or popularity.

Ever since 9/11 "nothing to hide" has been *the* thing to say. It is this kind of conditioned thinking that allows the Transportation Security Administration (TSA) to get by with ridiculously invasive searches that lack even a shred of "probable cause."

Just wait till this lady who is fine with CVS's "wellness" program—because she has nothing to hide—discovers that her a husband (or "partner") fell victim to an STD, thanks to a casual fling, and inadvertently gives it to *her*! Or her son, experimenting with homosexuality or drugs, contracts HIV, then shares glass of lemonade with Mom! Or, suppose this lady with nothing to hide discovers a genetic health problem that can be detected via DNA. Will an employer find an unrelated excuse to avoid hiring her?

This lady may suddenly discover she has a whole lot to hide and rue the day she said the *popular* thing on the air, no less, out of *fear* of appearing paranoid!

Citing **expertise** is another variation on the "appeal."

Because of the respect accorded the term "expert," it is easy to be misled. Behavioral and social "scientists," for example, are now deified by government, the courts, and the news media. Their word is taken for Gospel—even when they haven't any training or experience in the subject outside their area of specialty.

You will frequently hear lead-in phrases such as: "Child experts say. . . ."

Who are "child experts"? If I taught school for nine years, does that make me a "child expert"? Someone else may have majored in psychology and taken more courses in adolescent psychology than a teacher. But is he or she a "child expert"?

This line of reasoning constitutes an *appeal to expertise*. This does not mean that <u>some</u> teachers, psychiatrists or scientists—there's that "qualifying" term again—don't *say* the things attributed to them. They may, or may not.

But the problem, especially when facilitators and activists appeal to expertise, is that it is going to be used to justify, or build support for, whatever is coming <u>next</u>. An audience has no way of knowing, without checking, whether a *majority* of scientists, for example, believe that the Earth has warmed over the last one hundred years and caused the sea to rise.

Or, take that comment about low-self-esteem causing juvenile delinquency. Turns out that researchers with dual credentials in education and juvenile justice, such as Michael S. Brunner, was commission by the Justice Department to go into the juvenile detention system find out. Brunner found that most of the convicted minors had such high self-esteem that they thought—*really* thought—they could do almost anything, and that whatever they could <u>not</u> do (such as read passably), didn't matter anyway!

Sometimes an expert in one field is suddenly cited as an expert in another, especially if the person is well-known. Take the late Dr. Benjamin Spock, a celebrated (if not always agreed-with) pediatrician. During the Vietnam War, he became a spokesman for the anti-war movement. Indeed, he was treated as an expert on foreign affairs, which was not his field. Pediatrics was his field.

Now, you can hold any views you like on the Vietnam War, but the point is that Dr. Spock's achievements in pediatrics did not qualify him as an authority on foreign policy.

The same was true in the 1970s and '80s of actress Jane Fonda, with her anti-war and anti-nuclear activism. Or take today's superstar, Leonardo DiCaprio, on environmental causes!

Why should anyone care what celebrities think on topics for which they have zero background, have done no research and have taken little or no course work? Who cares that Bruce Springsteen supported John Kerry for President, or that Elton John supported George W. Bush? These are appeals to expertise and imply knowledge which these celebrities do not possess. Now, <u>if</u> a celebrity commits to independent research, or acquires verifiable, <u>non</u>-acting credentials, like former Sen. Fred Thompson, that's different.

Another appeal is best reflected in the statements "everybody does it." This is called an *"**appeal to common practice**."* Here, situational ethics kick in and moral benchmarks bow out.

Consider former US Rep. Anthony Weiner, who in 2011 tweeted a lewd photo involving his private parts, as well as other sexually explicit messages, and was pressured into resigning his position soon thereafter. But by 2013, he had decided that this lapse in judgment was a non-issue—enough so that he considered a run for New York mayor in 2014. And no wonder: Former President Bill Clinton, who "did not have sex with that woman, Monica Lewinsky" still garners hundreds of thousands of dollars in speaking engagements and sits on do-good boards with former President George H. W. Bush! The rationale for Mr. Weiner's new-found confidence, therefore, is found in the *appeal to common practice*—in this case, the intonation "everyone lies about sex."

SECTION 10

Questionable
Definitions

Let us move to the fallacy of **Ill-Defined Terms**. Frequently, the reason provocateurs get the upper hand at the outset of a discussion is because no one forces them to define their terms.

For example, education gurus of controversial curricula typically hail their programs as "progressive" or "cognitive." **Progressive** sounds like "progress" to modern minds, who don't recall John Dewey's revision of the term. Yet, that one change turned K–12 education into production mills of socialism.

Similarly, the term **cognitive** is commonly thought to mean solid, factual knowledge, when, in fact, it was changed in the 1980s to include *beliefs* and *attitudes*. In the federally funded Educational Resource Information Center (ERIC) repositories, there is a 1986 professional paper explaining the rationale for this, penned by James P. Shaver ("National Assessment of Values and Attitudes for Social Studies," pp. 5–6).

Most people who hear word **humanistic** mentally translate it as "humane." Highly educated persons may associate "humanistic" with Italian scholar and poet, Francesco Petrarca, who launched the humanist period in the arts during the Renaissance. Both versions carry positive connotations. Unfortunately, "humanistic *education*" is neither humane nor scholarly. So, what our opponents rely on, when they build their case around humanism, are people's *memories*—which can be dead wrong.

Another example is the term "adult entertainment," which has morphed into a triple "x" rating—or pornography. But real adult entertainment means something else, such as, a complex plot line in a TV drama, which is considered too difficult for children to follow, much less capture their interest on any long-term basis. These more sophisticated shows may be funny or serious, with maybe the occasional "off-color" joke or "double entendre."

The popular TV show, "The Good Wife" is actually a worthy example of real "adult entertainment." The screen writers did a fine job. Yes, there are the occasional references to homosexuality and non-marital liaisons and liberal political overtones. But the plot is constructed around <u>context</u>, with infrequent, graphic scenes that could just as well have been left.

The average fifteen-year-old would soon become bored with this show, due to its complexity. Only adults would be able to relate to themes like competing cutthroat law firms and hardball political-campaign management, which comprise the heart of the show. Watch it sometime. Whether you decide you like it or not, the show exemplifies a more realistic meaning of "adult entertainment," which is very unlike the exploding bodies, sexual sadism, or torture scenes of video gaming, replete with spines severed and little girls trapped and raped.

Summarizing Verbal and Psychological Combat

Before you even consider moving to the Advanced Course, you should be clear about principles that signal "verbal combat" and "psychological manipulation." So, remember the following information.

1. Know when you are under attack.
   A. If you cannot spot verbal aggression, you will be a perfect target.
   B. Do not assume you are "oversensitive," "paranoid," "reactionary," "narrow," or that you "just don't get it." If something doesn't sound right, there is probably a reason.

2. Know what kind of attack is being employed.
   A. Learn to identify the basic structures of fallacious reasoning.
   B. Learn to gauge the skill of your adversary and participants.

3. Make your defense appropriate to the attack.
   A. Remember that a stock response is not always the right one to use.
   B. Frequently the best defense is a good offense.

4. When targeted, always question the opponent's assumption(s) rather than taking the bait.

5. Follow through and play to win. Do not feel guilty about fighting back.
   A. This appears to be more difficult for women than for men.
   B. More husbands and fathers need to get into the fray instead of leaving it all to the women.

PRACTICE EXERCISES: DEFLECTING MANIPULATION

Drills and Rehearsals

Now that you have completed your study of the Beginner and Intermediate Courses, and have undertaken a cursory examination fallacious argument and reasoning, it's time to try some practice exercises, preferably with others.

Identify the provocation clause in each of the seven scenarios that follow; that is where you will find the red flag. (Wherever you see a portion between straight brackets [ ], that part can be replaced with virtually any topic.) You need to focus on the provocation, and that will allow you either to take on the topic at hand, or simply shut down the facilitator.

In **boldface, curly brackets { }** you will find commentaries by this author noting points for consideration or "class discussion," if you have a group of several participants in this practice session—which is highly recommended. Sometimes you will encounter enormous bloopers, and other times roaring successes. Occasionally there will be more than one way to respond, and you will see notations comparing "good responses" with either "alternate," or "better responses."

First, here's a warm-up: Recall that the best way to approach a smear is to treat it as a distraction, which, you may remember, is also an alienation strategy. Keep track of the specific topic you are on to avoid being trapped into debating a related or different one:

Facilitator: "Even a Christian extremist would admit *[that children need to protect themselves against sexually transmitted diseases.]*"

Poor Response:

"If you're saying I'm 'inflexible', and using that as the sole reason for my objections to your health curriculum, then you are not only being a bigot, but you're tainting my objection to suit yourself."

> *{Author comment: This is not a good response because you are being defensive and giving Facilitator a forum to continue attacking. You have not taken the reins of the debate.}*

Scenario 1: Psychological Screening Proposal [Requires 4]

Facilitator:

"In light of the rash of mass shootings, especially the one at Sandy Hook Elementary in Newtown, CT, we are looking at vastly expanding our mental-health services, including screening every student beginning in first grade, to identify mentally ill children and, if possible, prevent further such tragedies. I'd like to see the parents of this district be first to get behind this initiative so that others in the state will encourage legislators to move quickly state-wide."

Parent 1:

"Wait a minute. Everybody's privacy is being invaded enough as it is. Things kids say are taken out of context and blown up out of proportion. I don't want my child sent to a psychiatrist for aiming a chicken wing at another pupil."

Facilitator:

"We don't want to be victims of another Columbine or Virginia Tech, do we?"

Parent 2:

"How is asking pupils provocative questions going to prevent an incident?"

Facilitator:

"By identifying anti-social thoughts, we can flag kids for mental-health experts to take a second look and make a decision as to whether the child needs help."

Parent 1 (again):

"This sounds like a way to circumvent the family and take childrearing out of our hands."

Facilitator:

"Everyone here knows why <u>you</u> are against psychiatric intervention and screening."

Parent 1 (arguing forcefully):

"Whaddya mean, 'everyone here understands'? I resent your patronizing tone. Pretty soon, you'll be advocating that parents be hauled in for questioning!"

> *{Discuss before continuing: **Parent 1 has just given a terrible response. Why? Answer: Because she has provided Facilitator a means for ostracizing and marginalizing a critic.**}*

Facilitator:

"Well, it seems you tend to be a bit paranoid, and I think that's sort of reflected in your conspiracy-sounding comment about 'hauling parents in for questioning'. You must have a lot to hide"

Parent 2 (to the rescue of Parent 1):

"Wait a minute. I'm no conspiracy theorist, and I'm not against a person seeking the help of a psychiatrist. But I agree with the other lady. No one is consenting here—not the child or necessarily the parent. You are talking about school staff 'identifying' on the basis of a subjective survey or questionnaire that may or may not be prejudicial, and taking matters into its own hands"

Facilitator:

"Well, in some cases, that <u>might</u> actually be appropriate. Remember how the Virginia Tech shooter 'fell through the cracks' of Virginia's mental health system, because nobody bothered to follow up with parents and earlier counselors?"

Parent 3 (a new voice speaks up):

"How are these experts you refer to supposed to stop an Adam Lanza, Eric Harris or Dylan Klebold from harboring anti-social thoughts without immediately locking up every 'identified' pupil who yells at another child or gives the teacher a nasty look? Are you proposing to lock up, or drug, every kid who balks, or has a bad day? How many people here, including you, have never been angry about anything or stomped a foot in frustration?"

{Commentary: Parent 3's remarks succeed on three fronts: First, she plants seeds of doubt among the group when she refers to "locking up" and "drugging" kids; secondly, she offers real names, showing that she has a grasp of news events; and thirdly, she has taken hold of the reins of discussion by forcing Facilitator (and everyone else) to think about times when they were angry and, by implication, how that anger could be taken out of context.}

Scenario 2: New Sex Education Proposal

Parent: *"Sex education ought to be scrapped. It de-sensitizes a personal subject, much of the information is wrong, and kids don't learn real physiology."*

Board Member:

"That's a little extreme, don't you think? It's the responsibility of society to see that children learn about sex. Surely you'll agree that children need information that doesn't come off the street."

Parent:

"Of course, but the schools are not providing that."

Board Member:

"Sex is a very important topic and an integral part of life. Don't you think that sex is important for every child?"

{Oops! Board Member changed the subject. Will Parent catch her on it?}

Parent:

"Of course, it's important. That's why the schools shouldn't teach it!"

{Gotcha! Hooray for Parent!}

Scenario 3: Money for School Computers Proposal

Parent:

"A budget agreement that calls for even more federal funding for education is absolutely wrong-headed. No matter how much money is appropriated, it is never enough, and too much is spent on non-academic matters."

Facilitator:

"But it's vital that kids have state-of-the-art equipment to be well-educated today, and that's expensive. This is the Information Age, after all."

Parent:

"High-technology is no more vital to elementary reading, spelling, addition and subtraction than a lamp shade."

> **{Oops! Parent made a poor analogy here, and comes close to distracting any friends in the audience.}**

Facilitator:

"High-technology is vital to everyone nowadays. You have a computer at home, don't you? Don't you think your child will also need one in the future for work?"

Parent:

"Many will. But high technology is not the primary thing educators are spending money on; and secondly, basic subjects like arithmetic don't require them. In fact, computers can be a distraction."

> **{Aah! Parent gets back on the subject and Facilitator didn't catch the gaffe.}**

Scenario 4: The Hysterical Debater

No-Grades Activist:

"Grades should be discouraged. Students should progress in school subjects at their own pace, with remedial help available. That way no child is pressured by senseless competition but, rather, is encouraged to understand the material. Curriculum is not a sport."

Parent Debater:

"If we did that, kids would stay in fourth-grade math class until they're thirty years old!"

No-Grades Activist:

"What are you so uptight about? I don't want to do away with competition <u>entirely</u>; I just think making school subjects boil down to grades early on is counter-productive."

Parent Debater:

"How do you expect this nation to be competitive if pupils never compete for anything important? Competitiveness is key to our economy. When you undercut competition, you risk this nation's economic survival, unless you're so in love with the idea of interdependence that you've lost interest in economic survival."

No-Grades Activist:

"Who said anything about interdependence? You're twisting everything I say."

{Discussion Question: **Parent is losing this one, and comes across as hysterical. What <u>changes</u> might have saved Parent's argument? Isn't the following what this Parent actually meant to say, but under pressure and flustered, did not?**}

ANSWER: Alternative, Improved Parent Response:

*"How do you expect this nation to be competitive if pupils never compete for anything **except sports**? **Benchmarks** are key to our economy. When you undercut **grading scales**, you risk the nation's economic edge unless you've bought into the globalist notion "about **leveling the playing field**" and have lost interest in this nation's **high standard of living**."*

Scenario 5: Hasty Generalization and Changed Subject

Lynn:

"I think all this self-esteem stuff is garbage."

Brett:

"What do you mean?"

Lynn:

"Well, like inventing historical facts to inflate African-American egos. According to some curriculums, the roots of Western civilization are in Africa, and Napoleon deliberately shot off the nose of the Sphinx to alter its facial features so people wouldn't know it was African. Not only that, but Cleopatra supposedly was black according to some version of Acts in the Bible. Yet, several scholars point out that Cleopatra <u>died</u> way before that book of the Bible was written. The Ptolemies were known to prefer <u>Greek</u> wives and mistresses, so surly ancient writers would have recorded that Cleopatra had an African ancestor if she'd had one!"

Brett:

"Well, I have to admit, those examples seem a little off base."

Lynn:

"Like I said, all this self-esteem nonsense is absolutely nuts."

> **{Oops! Oversimplification and generalization here! Will Brett pick up on it?}**

Brett:

"Hold it. I agree with you on the examples you cited. But I didn't say I thought <u>all</u> self-esteem was nuts. Afrocentric curriculum doesn't represent the entire self-esteem movement. Besides, don't you think it's important not to demoralize kids in school?"

> **{Yes, Brett nailed Lynn, BUT, in doing so, he <u>changed the subject</u> with his "demoralizing kids" comment!}**

Lynn:

"Who said anything about 'demoralizing'? That's another subject. Demoralizing someone means going <u>out your way</u> to embarrass and belittle a person."

> **{Lynn nailed Brett, too, but nothing was accomplished by the whole argument.}**

Scenario 6: Choosing one's words carefully

Health Clinic Rep.:

"Look, we're talking about raging hormones here. There's no point in injecting pious morality into this issue."

Parent:

"In other words, their instincts, as though they have no control over behavior."

Health Clinic Rep.:

"I told you I wasn't going to debate morality. We are talking about drives that are common to <u>all</u> animal species."

Parent:

"If that is so, then perhaps you can explain to me why all the 'other animals' don't need condoms."

> {Commentary: Health Clinic Rep. just handed Parent a fantastic opening by using the oversimplified and poorly defined term "all animal species." Even so, why was it imperative that Parent respond with the word "need," instead of saying "use." (Just think about it, before someone gets laughed out of the room!) Thus, the need for practice sessions.}

Scenario 7: The "Gotcha" Moment (12 people required)

> {THINK as you review this one: Which Principle of Psych War does this entire dialogue most represent? Three questions, including this one, will be asked at the conclusion.}

Focus Group Team Member 1:

"I don't need to worry about my daughter becoming an HIV statistic."

Change Agent:

"Oh? And why is that?"

Team Member 1 (again):

"Because I've taught her right from wrong; that sex is a sacred trust based on love and commitment, not about gross diseases."

Team Member 2:

"I agree. I'm teaching my daughter to grow up to be a moral individual."

Team Member 3:

"I feel that way, too, because I think it's important to preserve childhood innocence instead of stealing it."

Team Member 4:

"Many parents here feel that today's parenting advice is ill-conceived."

{Question: What words did Team Members 4 & 5 use to gain advantage? Answer: "Many of us"; "Most of us."}

Team Member 5:

"Most of us believe that sex is a private matter, not a subject to be plastered in front of the room like a billboard, especially in a classroom setting."

Team Member 6:

"It's not right to treat our kids as if they were brought up on the street."

Team Member 7:

"I think the best way to avoid unwanted pregnancies and STDs is to teach abstinence till marriage."

Change Agent (discouraged by the comments so far):

"OK. What can we do, then, besides (or in addition to) offering abstinence as a way to avoid unwanted pregnancy to our junior high school students?"

Team Member 8 – Melanie (who hasn't spoken yet):

"Maybe we need more comprehensive sex education programs."

{Suddenly, Change Agent will brighten a bit}

Team Member 9: (eagerly and excitedly)

"Yes. Let's find some pregnant teenagers and have them address the elementary-school children."

{Team Members 8-12, all applaud, (inc. Melanie!)}

Team Member 10: (also eagerly & excitedly)

"I know! Let's show films of male and female genitals infected with herpes."

{Team Members 8-12, all nod "yes," (inc. Melanie!)}

Team Member 11: (also eagerly & excitedly)

"We could also mandate genital exams for all six-year-olds by school nurses to check for signs of STDs—and advise Child Protective Services of possible sexual abuse, too, all in one swoop."

{Team Members 8-12, all agree noisily, (inc. Melanie!) again.}

Team Member 12: (also eagerly & excitedly)

"Hang posters in the hallways about making condoms more attractive!"

{Team Members 8-12, all agree noisily (inc. Melanie!) again.}

Change Agent (really warming to her new-found allies):

"All right. All right. You guys have done some great brainstorming. Let's examine these ideas. What do you think about a pilot program with the local university to bring in college students who've <u>had</u> an STD to discuss their experience with the sixth-grade class next month? I'm sure the department would be helpful about getting volunteers."

{Change Agent continues, ignoring (turning away from) the first 7 Team Members, and playing up to the others}:

"Suppose we implement a trial program in elementary schools with a new film demonstrating proper use of condoms on human mock-ups, for just three months?"

{Team Member <u>8</u> (Melanie, the first among the pro-comprehensive sex ed participants), raises her hand, <u>knowing</u> she will be acknowledged. (Question: How does she know this?)}

Change Agent [pleasantly and politely]:

"Yes, Melanie. Your thoughts?"

Team Member 8, Melanie:

"You know, I'm having second thoughts. The only really effective means of reducing unwed pregnancy and STDs is to have a monogamous relationship within marriage. I think we ought to be discussing the various abstinence education programs out there. How many abstinence programs have you brought for us to review?"

Change Agent (AGHAST & AT A LOSS FOR WORDS):

{No comment.}

Now, answer these three discussion questions that all relate to scenario 7:

1. Which Principle of Psych-War does this scenario represent?

2. What words did Team Members 4 & 5 use to gain an initial advantage?

3. What made Melanie (Team Member 8) so sure she her final question will be readily acknowledged by the change agent?

Answer 1: "Recruit persons who are highly intelligent, but can appear stupid; who can play dumb, but are in reality strong; who are principled, but can appear passive; who are willing to be humiliated to succeed."

Answer 2: "Many of us"; "Most of us".

Answer 3: Because Melanie already said what the change agent wanted to hear earlier.

Take a break before moving on to the more difficult Advanced Course!

ADVANCED COURSE— HARDBALL ATTACK STRATEGIES

Introduction

A headline opinion piece by feature writer Steven Pearlstein March 15, 2013, captured the essence of today's post 20th-century American mindset when he wrote "Is Capitalism Moral?" for the *Washington Post*. It was worth the read. The piece hit the high points of both conservative and liberal arguments concerning socialism versus free-based markets. But the title question would never have been openly asked in America prior to 1960. Even President Franklin D. Roosevelt would have kept the question concerning the morality of capitalism to himself.

The fact is, our nation has come a long way in its acceptance of socialism. Modern middle-class "entitlements," such as Social Security, Medicare and subsidized college loans are like the garbage disposal in your kitchen: They're so pervasive that virtually no one can imagine life without them.

That, of course, was the point of initiating them. Once even the middle class got hooked, socialism was in the bag, along with a more heavy-handed government, required to enforce the massive numbers of regulations that social programs entail.

Of course, there still are a few self-made millionaires, and even the most totalitarian countries have them. They are tolerated, to a greater or lesser degree, to keep the elite in power and the country afloat. A notable exception would be North Korea.

In the United States, folks like Mitt Romney really *did* earn their own fortunes. But his age (a first-wave baby boomer, born in 1947) represents a cut-off point between old-school upbringing and the "progressive" philosophy.

While his father, George, was a wealthy executive with a lot of self-made friends, colleagues (and, later, political ties), young Mitt was not allowed to live off the largesse his famous parents. Brought up in what is now deemed an old-fashioned ethic, he tarnished his 2012 presidential campaign with utterances about the 47 percent of Americans who, by paying no taxes and relying *primarily* on government support, are virtual wards of today's creeping welfare state. These people, he knew, were not appropriate targets for his campaign, which centered on the traditional American work ethic. Correct or not, voicing such sentiments anywhere near a microphone is politically incorrect.

Asking whether capitalism is moral, on the other hand, is acceptable—even if the term "capitalism" does not exactly capture the essence of the Founders' free-market vision but, rather, was popularized much later. In fact, it was coined as a pejorative by mid-nineteenth century socialists to denote rich bosses ("fat cats") who exploit workers (employees) for personal profit. By the time the Cold War was in full swing, the ideals of economic individualism, self-reliance and self-sufficiency had mostly given way (at least in the media and under President Lyndon B. Johnson) to "economic equality" and "abolishing poverty." After a brief resurgence of a "financial independence" model during the Reagan Administration (two of President Ronald Reagan's own children publicly mocked everything this model stood for), in which many struggled to turn back the siren song of welfare and egalitarianism, the brief reprieves for economic autonomy soon vanished—except on paper. Even then, high regulation and punishing taxation made it tough for wannabe entrepreneurs to move into the "self-made" category.

Romney's upbringing was a hangover from a fading era when young people, regardless of family means or background, were expected to make their own way once they were out of the nest.

The famous clan related to John F. Kennedy, by contrast, had long since dropped any chatter that upheld the peculiar American ethic about self-reliance. The late Teddy Kennedy, in particular, pushed hard for socialism "for the masses," as if such were the norm, and free markets an aberration.

The Kennedys, like many of our nation's leaders by the late 1960s, unconsciously leaned toward the side of elitism—that is, a European-style, privileged class. Thus, they saw no irony in pushing a welfare state, and would have found no hypocrisy in asking whether "capitalism" is moral.

Well, we all know what happened to Mitt Romney. Ironically, he found himself castigated in the media—and therefore, by average Americans—for the same elitism *his* father's ilk (George Romney) would have showered on the liberals of his own day.

Moreover, a sea-change in attitudes concerning all sorts of questions—not just economics—is impacting even the concept of "morality" itself, especially among teenagers and young voters, thanks mainly to the schools. This places American constitutionalists and traditionalists in an awkward position.

On the one hand, we like to say that economic success derives from hard work, ingenuity (or, if you prefer, thinking outside-the-box), a rigorous education, and a market system that rewards both virtue and experience, no matter one's background. On the other, we are confronted with a paradox: In an odd twist on the "old boy network," which divvied out alliances, perks and favoritism (even to a few women), a new and grossly manipulative "network" of political preference and prejudice emerged to replace it.

One must still have the right combination of parents and schools—only, this time around, it belongs to a "protected minority," or is classified by public schools and the Census Bureau as befitting a particular socio-economic stereotype of poverty, cultural disadvantage or (incredulously) extreme wealth—of the Warren Buffett, Bill Gates variety. The upward mobility concept is disappearing; the "middle class" being the Biggest Losers. Its bourgeois values and hard-work ethic don't bring them the advantage of scholarships, special-deal "loans," or smoothed pathways by which to take over the family business when elders pass on.

Thus, if you have the wealth of a George Soros, Donald Trump, Bill Gates, Oprah Winfrey, Michael Bloomberg, or perhaps a great "throwing arm" in football that bestows a proverbial "leg up" for you and your children, you won't necessarily win access to elite Party hacks who rise to head the most important committees and subcommittees in government.

So maybe Pearlstein was right when he suggested in his article on the morality of capitalism that success and wealth today are mostly a matter of "dumb luck."

Moreover, "the American Dream" is morphing into the pervasive notion that Government has a *responsibility* to create a "default outcome." Not just a "fallback" position, as in *safety net*, but a *default* setting, as with a computer. Social programs, government projects and various redistributions of wealth are the norm, not the exception. Anything <u>above</u> that is considered a "lucky" bonus. Anyone who doesn't adhere to this new concept of "what's fair" is going to be attacked, whether the topic is schools, the environment, housing, foreign policy, crime or health care.

SECTION 1

From Personal Attacks to "Broad Strokes"

The last few years has brought a vast increase in what are called "attack publications," published by the Left to teach its own political wing how to rebuff criticism on a large scale, not just from any remaining conservatives, constitutionalists or traditionalists who happen to appear at meetings, on committees and in focus groups. What they are after is broad, inflammatory swipes against any group or faction that could gain a toe-hold on the public scene and influence others. The tremendous popularity of Ronald Reagan in 1982 was a wakeup call to the Left that a charismatic conservative, with some established credibility, could still force the left-wing to regroup instead of forging ahead in the manner to which it had become accustomed. Even though the Left did, in fact, ultimately prevail and forge ahead, the possibilities still scared them, and the rush was on to create more front groups, to recruit more change agents and train more professional manipulators.

Among the prolific sources of pamphlets, manuals, booklets, flyers and workshops aimed at deflecting traditionalists and patriots are the National Education Association, along with its state chapters and political spin-offs, such as UniServ. Other sources are connected to so-called environmental and "sustainable development" policy groups—especially Agenda 21, which is a United Nations construct with action plans specializing in left-wing environmentalism and city planning issues worldwide.

Then there are ubiquitous organizations like the Education Commission of the States and the American Civil Liberties Union with their daggers always out; and the American Planning Association, of course, is busy foisting redistribution of wealth under the cover of "city planning."

Institutes, Associations, Foundations, and NGOs

Add to these, hundreds of "helpful" left-leaning institutes, associations, foundations and "Centers" for This-and-That: all of them financially secure, and frequently contributing to each other's causes. Many receive grants and contracts via government as well as from still other household-name organizations, such as the Carnegie, Ford, Johnson, and Rockefeller Foundations or from the likes of the American Humanist Association. Specific ones may borrow money back and forth in a pinch; and many work through universities (which may *themselves* benefit from still other government grants and foundation endowments).

Moreover, thousands of organizations are lumped together as *non-governmental organizations* (or "NGOs"). The Nation's Capital is home to some 1,300 NGOs; New York has around 1,000. Many were launched by long-deceased philanthropists—and well before the burden of taxes. So, many stay in their headquarter buildings tax-free.

NGOs are the nesting places for academics, politicians, former ambassadors, do-gooders, busy-bodies and the occasional maniac. Some NGOs benefit indirectly from state and/or federal government grants and contracts simultaneously, which can get dicey, especially if one of them finds itself on the wrong side of political correctness.

In a republic like ours, power equals influence. Unelected power lies in the ability to influence elections (when that even matters anymore)— but more significantly, they can mobilize public opinion through a combination of slick marketing and lobbying. Most hire professional public relations groups or "consultants," all of whom know a great deal about something we alluded to earlier—perception management.

A sophisticated form of bribery is the charitable "donation" or "contribution," from which some sort of return is expected. If an NGO becomes powerful enough, its influence may require no more than what is known as "the quiet word"—a piece of well-placed advice to an office-holder or policymaker.

Sample NGOs

- Open Society Institute
- The National Education Association & state and local affiliates
- The American Civil Liberties Union
- Americans for Separation of Church and State

- Americans for Religious Liberty
- The National Coalition Against Censorship
- The Carnegie Foundation for the Advancement of Teachers
- The Rockefeller Foundation
- The Danforth Foundation
- The Ford Foundation
- The Aspen Institute for Humanistic Studies
- The Kettering Foundation
- The Robert Wood Johnson Foundation
- The Association for Supervision and Curriculum Development
- The National Council for Social Studies
- The American Library Association
- The American Association of School Administrators
- The Freedom to Read Foundation
- The National School Boards Association
- The World Population Council
- Lesbian, Gay, Bisexual, and Transgender Network
- Coalition for Democracy
- Coalition for Choice
- American Humanist Association

More critical is that many of these organizations help launch curricula. These help indoctrinate upcoming generations into an anti-parent, anti-religion, anti-morality, redistribution-of-wealth mindset. They also serve to prepare teachers to expect "nutty" parents who criticize policies and programs, and to warn likeminded colleagues of any "conservative" locals thinking of running for school boards (an entire section is devoted later in this course to the incredible level of attack that goes into defeating traditionalist school board candidates). This gives the Left a psychological leg up, and most parents know nothing about it.

Constitutionalists and other specialized conservative organizations (i.e., those associated with fiscal issues, social issues, Second Amendment and family issues) do exist, of course, but they *compete* for funds rather than share them. They are typically strapped for cash, and have nowhere near the networking capabilities and skills (nor frankly, the interest) in launching the kind of meaningful resistance that the Left engages in on a regular basis.

School administrators get a particularly hard-hitting version of anti-traditionalist indoctrination, which is one reason this course spends so much time on education. Each new class of high school and college graduates moves increasingly toward the Left, and the lion's share of the reason is teacher preparation and the courses taken by prospective school administrators. Occasionally teachers become tired of the classroom environment and take additional classes at the local arm of a university to move into more lucrative administrative posts. It requires a number of courses to get there; so most school administrators go into management from the beginning and spend little or no time in a classroom actually teaching youngsters.

Whereas prior to around 1958, school administrators tended to view themselves as a teacher's backup and support system, thanks to the teachers unions (the NEA and, to a lesser extent, the American Federation of Teachers), since that time teachers and administrators have adopted a more adversarial position, as in "the workers" versus "managers" or "superiors."

Targeting School Administrators

Today's school administrators, such as principals and superintendents, tend to see teachers as "the hired help," with a responsibility to make principals, superintendents and school districts in general look good in the media. This "responsibility" does not extend to ensuring that pupils leave school with factual knowledge. It means appeasing and entertaining kids so they will stay in school, off the street, and be reasonably compliant while they are being warehoused.

This means bolstering test scores in any way possible, including ensuring that educators virtually "teach the test," such as it is, and look the other way when teachers inflate pupils' grades (with a thinly veiled threat that poor pupil performance will adversely affect teacher evaluations, regardless of the reason). All this is part of community public relations. So, it is no wonder when even in some of the most highly taxed communities in the country (such as Montgomery County, Maryland, a suburb of Washington, D.C.), a majority of students fail their final exams in math and other subjects, as happened in 2013.

Whenever a scandal to the effect that teachers have "helped" students on tests, or changed their grades, emerges in the media (e.g., in Atlanta, Georgia, 2013), administrators blame teachers, not policies. So, it's no wonder that the teachers unions are able to pit teachers against administrators from the get-go, and rake in big bucks from mandatory "collective bargaining," even though many teachers disagree with leftist union politics. After all, principals and superintendents aren't exactly *right*-wing, as we shall discover in some of the course work aimed at them, samplings from which are provided in these pages.

Why Schools are Microcosms of Shifting America Loyalties

Moreover, agencies and organizations aligned with the education establishment scratch one another's back on some issues, such as tests and grades, while otherwise maintaining a strained and hostile working relationship between employers (administrators) and employees (teachers and support staff). The holds particularly for federal agencies directors are pitted against civil-service bureaucrats, resulting in today's unionized lower- and mid-level bureaucracies that stay on from one political administration to the next.

As for K–12 institutions, teachers complain they don't get any backup from their administrators (true, at least as instructors in academics), and administrators complain teachers are incompetent (also increasingly true). This leaves educators who are truly learned and conscientious facing an uphill battle; they are assigned the worst classes and given the least support, in the hope that they will either quit or retire early.

It is important to understand that this combative relationship has been carefully orchestrated over decades. A built-in hostility has been inculcated between "workers" and "management" that smacks of Karl Marx, Vladimir Lenin, Josef Stalin, and a long list of other infamous socialists and communists.

That is why the "education establishment" serves as a microcosm of what is happening in other venues throughout America, such as law enforcement (e.g., police commissioners and mayors versus average cops). Once you understand how the agenda behind course work at all levels—K–12, college undergraduate and graduate-level—the predicaments you encounter elsewhere, even in houses of worship, become clearer.

The increasing reticence of US schools to teach factual information in history, economics, science, and logic has made it particularly easy to miss the differences between our American Founders' vision of representative democracy, and the European-socialist view. Gaps in the public knowledge base help accelerate the trend of legitimizing non-binding, feel-good resolutions, similar to those that emanate from foreign interest groups (including the United Nations). These become intertwined with local and state laws and soon pervade society.

We will be taking up three samples of "attack literature," the best examples emanating from the educational setting. These examples enjoy a certain "transfer value" to other realms, ranging from local environmental policy changes, to citizen complaints on just about any topic you can name.

The attack materials cited here keep being updated, and sometimes are even retitled, but the basics remain the same—as do the Principles of Psych War we learned in the Beginner Course. The following publications, therefore, serve to demonstrate the utter viciousness of your opponents and nail down specific tactics so that you can chart a course for stemming the worst of them. Three representative attack training booklets are:

1. The first attack publication was part of a course for prospective school administrators by Richard P. Manatt with Guest Writer Joe Drips, International Journal of Education Reform. Now retitled, was used as required reading for education administration course (Ed. Ad. 541) at Iowa State University, Ames, Iowa, as far back as 1993: "The Attack by the US Religious Right on 'Government Schools'," subtitled "Who was that masked man who stole our education reform?" Hereafter, this text will be referred to as the *Manatt/Drips course.*

2. The second attack publication is entitled "What's Left After the Right? A Resource Guide for Educators," by Janet L. Jones, Ed.D., for the Washington Education Association, a state chapter of (and funded by) the National Education Association. It was launched in 1986, (195 pages) and morphed over the years into a manual for activists. It will be referred to, again in abbreviated form, as the Washington State *NEA manual.*

3. "How to Deal With Community Criticism of School Change" is a joint publication of the NEA spin-off organization, the Association for Supervision and Curriculum Development (ASCD) and a Carnegie Foundation spin-off, the Education Commission of the States (ECS), 1993 (hereafter, the *ASCD/ECS handbook*).

SECTION 2

"Attack" Publications

Attack publications are noteworthy not only for what they state, but for what they omit; for their use of "smears" (a.k.a. "black PR"), and for distortions of fact. They also help us—*when* they reflect what their writers *honestly* believe—to comprehend our opponents' prejudices.

For example, in a glossary of terms found in the Manatt/Drips course for school administrators, it states that the Religious Right (which includes everybody who takes exception to a school policy, curriculum, text, program, or activity) opposes "multicultural studies" programs. The newest controversial curriculum making the rounds today is called a "white privilege" unit. In this one, some pupils must wear bracelets labeled "white and privileged." Anybody having even a passing familiarity with World War II history might be reminded of armbands embossed with the Star of David that were a required accessory to be worn by Jewish inhabitants in Nazi Germany.

Speaking of which, it was reported by Tim Devaney in a March 18, 2013, column for the Washington Times ("Lessons in How to Hate from Experts: Nazis, Klan Speak at Schools") that some public schools, including a few in Columbus, Ohio, and Topeka, Kansas, had invited pre-labeled "hate-groups"—ostensibly to teach "critical thinking skills." Among the invitees were neo-Nazi organizations and the Ku Klux Klan—which amazingly, still have followings. Such groups are supposed to air their views, while pupils listen politely, without "reacting," in the spirit of a democracy. The superficial message is: "At least try to understand where people you don't necessarily agree with are coming from."

Sounds reasonable, doesn't it? But things go a bit off-kilter when they bring pro-life advocates, same-sex "marriage" detractors, and representatives of various anti-welfare groups into classrooms for the same purpose.

Think: *Can you explain what's "off" about this?*

ANSWER: Without specifically saying so, traditional values have been added with the "hate-group" tag. Thus, anything can be labeled "radical" at any time. It's real subtle, because the kids are being told to *listen* to everyone. But a subliminal message also is inserted. According to the *Washington Times* report, this class activity in Ohio has been ongoing since the 1970s, introduced as "US Political Thought and Radicalism," which implies (because of the date) that leftist sources originated the program.

Prospective school administrators who get involved in programs like these also learn in preparatory course work, such as the Manatt/Drips school administration curriculum that the real source of economic success derives *not* from hard work, but from "economics, languages, governments, and ecosystems worldwide." However, unlike twenty years ago, there are few, or no, materials to back up this claim: No references to the tomes of revered globalists like James Becker (editor of *Schooling for a Global Age*, McGraw-Hill, 1979), who believed, among other things, that humans are "the most destructive of all animals"; nothing from John Goodlad's 1984 watershed text (also published by McGraw-Hill), *A Place Called School*, pointing to educational facilities as launch pads for socialism; and no quotations from Benjamin Bloom, author of *Taxonomy of Educational Objectives* (1956, updated 1978), who asserted that the purpose of education was "to challenge children's fixed beliefs," not to transmit knowledge.

So, either the course's creators, Manatt nd Drips, really didn't know why traditionalistic Americans criticize "multicultural studies," or they knew but didn't care to present the whole story, preferring instead to create a negative, knee-jerk reaction toward stereotypical "conservative" critics.

Nearly everything that falls into the category of an "attack publication" is aimed at ensuring that communities, workplaces and schools deflect "conservative" criticism. They squelch controversy on issues ranging from "sustainable development," to government-subsidized health care, to transgendered classrooms, to ethanol-overload in your fuel tank—then suggest that any public disapproval is the result of *theology* (of all things!) running amok. This notion is an ever-easier sell in a post-9/11 world, where real fanatics commit bizarre suicide missions in the name of their god.

September 11 was a game-changer in more ways than one. The Left now believes it can once-and-for-all sever links to Judeo-Christian morality, beginning with Christianity-based ethics in schools which, according to religion-bashers, too easily spills over into the public forum. The Left has already succeeded in removing the remnants of religious expressions—from changing actual tenets of the Faith, to challenging as unconstitutional the long-standing use of Christian churches as venues for important occasions and events like graduation ceremonies, to tearing down war memorials on public lands (such as highways) that incorporate Christian icons, to re-naming anything once associated with religious holidays—"Easter vacation" is now "Spring Break," and "Happy Holidays" replaces "Merry Christmas."

Characterizations of anti-Left Critics

In general, the "God-and-country" branch of anti-Left critics are characterized as "extremists," "out-of-touch," "loners" and "individualistic" folks (as opposed to the politically correct preference for "team players"). Anybody with a penchant for traditional values is lumped together with people who want to "go back to 1950s." The 1950s era is today almost universally interpreted as an era of bigotry and racism, with only the rare allusion to this period as being one of great optimism, high commitment to family and producing the highest standard of living on earth.

Frequent Smears

- Far-Right, Radical Right (replaces "Moral Majority")
- Self-styled patriots and Nationalists
- Knuckle-draggers
- Ultra-Conservatives
- Christians and/or Christian Fundamentalists
- Censors
- Lunatic Fringe

Critics are increasingly labeled "enemies"—of public education, of conservation, of the planet, of minorities: whatever the topic *du jour* happens to be. These should be treated as blatant oversimplifications (as per the intermediate-level course). Nothing much is said about these supposed "enemies" being opposed to a socialist, welfare state, or to an increasingly acceptance of corruption and moral turpitude. This, of course, would more accurately depict the breadth and scope of American "conservatism," but doing so would also give our side a "human face"—the very thing Saul Alinsky admonished his followers against, for strategic reasons.

For the most part, writers of attack manuals base their smears on the writings and presentations of the *most* strident and *least* articulate among traditionalist-conservative critics, using such individuals as catch-all stereotypes. Well-spoken and highly respected commentators/ columnists become *verboten*—even those once associated with the liberal-left camp: For example, the incomparable comedian, Bill Cosby, who once marched for civil rights; Dr. Ben Carson, the renowned neurosurgeon who thrived under the strict tutelage of his then-young, teenage, single mother; and Tammy Bruce, the open lesbian who lambasted the gay movement for its hypocrisy. These are just a few of the "heretics" who have found themselves marginalized, merely for taking issue with one or two favorite leftist mantras.

"The World We Live In"?

Only rarely are specific criticisms by conservatives quoted and rebutted, point by point. And that's a red flag! Another less-noticed red flag that traditionalists, constitutionalists and conservatives allow to pass without a challenge, is the oft-repeated justification by the Left for increasingly draconian regulations and new laws: "This is the world we live in today!"

In truth, today's America is the world the Left has <u>allowed</u> to emerge over a forty-five-year period! (Recall: "Create a crisis and impose the solution," Beginner Course.) Prior to the 1960s, our populace did not require impossible-to-open bottle caps and scissor-defying shrink-wrap on medications and foods. In the "awful" 1950s, there was no need for chain-link fencing on over-street bridges and crossways (to stem the dropping of hard objects onto cars beneath), double and triple locks on average homes, and all sorts of other time-consuming nuisances.

Does it ever occur to our younger leftist opposition *why* we have so many villains randomly targeting routinely purchased products? Most of those caught tampering with and hurling dangerous objects have long rap sheets today. But it was childrearing advice to parents and student disciplinary codes in schools *after* the 1960s that "created the conditions" (see "The Rules of Psych War," Beginner Course), for "the world we live in." Yesterday's "dangerous mischief" has escalated to bombs and mass shootings by out-of-control brats. These conditions have been exacerbated via Step 2 of the Five Steps to Indoctrination (section 4, Beginner Course):

Bombard the subject's senses with a steady diet of conflicting, contradictory and confusing images and words . . . in order to discourage reflection.

A few of the more hypocritical "conditions" that most will recognize, if they think about it, were mentioned in an April 2013 *Washington Times* article by Victor Davis Hanson of the Hoover Institution:

- portrayals of nicotine and cigarettes "a corporate-sponsored, unclean and dirty habit that leads to long-term health costs for society. . .," while simultaneously characterizing marijuana ("pot" or "weed") as trendy, even downright medicinal;
- regularly (and almost mandatorily) inclusion of graphic language, simulated sexual intercourse and nude scenes into every possible TV venue and popular novel, while concurrently mandating a zero-tolerance policy "for casual banter and slang in the media or the workplace" under the cover of sexual harassment;
- curricular university "elective" courses in prostitution, perversion and pornography, while at the same time encouraging lawsuits over "hurtful" (politically incorrect) terminologies applied to "protected" factions of society: such as, women (*ladies*), homosexuals (*fags, perverts*); the African-American race (*Negroes*); non-widowed, single parents (*illegitimacy*); and promiscuous individuals (*sluts, escorts*).

No wonder young Americans have inherited a vacuum where a belief system used to be!

Moreover, once-liberal (and even *still*-liberal) critics, if they dare speak out, often have <u>no idea</u> why they are now being sidelined or rejected by their former comrades!

SECTION 3

Who Do Our Opponents Think They Are?

According to the Manatt/Drips course in school administration all critics of educational programs, policies, or curriculums are "salt of the earth, concerned parents and/or community members"; but unfortunately are also "absolutists." It is this absolutism which supposedly makes all of us intolerant and inflexible in our beliefs. Absolutism is seen as a mental disorder that must be abolished—and, of course the Left determines what actions and thoughts fall under the absolutist definition. Our opponents further allege that conservative critics are usually members of "ultra-conservative, fundamentalist, charismatic or Pentecostal faiths"; affiliated with "Far Right" organizations; and "[w]illing to devote . . . weeks, months and years to their cause" (as *if* the Left is not).

Your "working opposition" on the Left, however, sees itself as "voices of reason," or, as the NEA manual states:

> "[p]ersons with a . . . moderate perspective [who] believe that public education is an essential societal entity through which children of all ethnic groups and religious (or non-religious) persuasions, learn to think creatively, productively and critically. . . [and] who promote a diverse curriculum that provides children with the mental tools by which they may survive and compete in a . . . changing world."

This comes across as sensible, upbeat, and open-minded. Remember that the NEA supposedly speaks for school-age children (and of course their teachers), which puts the emphasis here on youngsters. The Left has always attempted to co-opt public opinion via the youngest members of society, who have no experience and are, in effect, a "captive audience." Never mind that many children don't "survive" the public school at all, and that since the basic tools for *intellectual* survival, such as reading, writing and math, get such short shrift, our economy (and the students' financial future) are now in danger.

Most significantly, our left-leaning "working opposition" sees itself as "committed to excellence . . . educat[ing] the whole person to be a caring, involved citizen of a global society."

But recall that professional papers out of the US Dept. of Education began viewing "excellence" as a flawed concept in the 1970s, and made it official in 1981 in a policy paper by two top-tier staffers, Archie LaPointe and Willard Wirtz. The paper, "Measuring the Quality of Education," also coined the term *functional literacy* to describe education's new goal. The expression stuck. They highlighted instead social interconnection, and promoted progressive educational theories as "child-centered." Today, they are more correct than they ever imagined at the time: Today's youngsters tend to remain emotional adolescents forever.

First and foremost, our adversaries characterize themselves as "Friends of Education," and even "liberals," but never as leftists or as cooperating with ideological regulators working toward a statist-style government.

A note of caution here: It is important to recognize that ***not*** all of our adversaries, including some of those on our earlier long list of left-wing (and/or non-governmental) organizations, are "co-conspirators." Some have been drawn <u>into</u> the Illiteracy Cartel—either because they have been conditioned and indoctrinated, or because they are no longer particularly well-educated on the roots of their various "causes" and "missions." Time has moved on; the boat sailed.

The current crop of activists (post-60s) probably could not tell you anything about the writings of John Dewey, his alliances or his supporters. They couldn't recap the philosophies of Benjamin Bloom or school testing-*cum*-assessment guru Ralph Tyler, much less the contributions of key Marxist organizers like Antonio Gramsci or Herbert Marcuse. They have no memory of the Cold War-era training that went into organizing the campus protests, riots and demonstrations of the 1960's, such as the PITs (<u>P</u>assable <u>I</u>nfiltration <u>T</u>eams), that were taught to blend in with local populations, picking up the trends, colloquialisms and mannerisms needed to seduce an emerging generation of voters, corporate moguls, educators and bureaucrats. Yet, these techniques are the very ones taught to youngish change-agent recruits, such as those of the American Planning Association, alluded to earlier. The goal was to produce, within a generation, individuals who had fully "internalized" the dogma of political correctness. And they did!

Unfortunately, the PITs succeeded, and both they and their offspring stayed on, redefining American values and effectively minimizing Western culture under the cover of upgrading Third World societies (which, unsurprisingly, remain largely unchanged).

Most people today feel busier and more overwhelmed than their 1950s-era forebears, due in large part to the intrusiveness of electronic gadgets and social media that, in effect, never leaves them alone with their thoughts. Younger Americans are "connected" 24/7, and even most adults under the age of sixty-five will tell you plainly that forgetting to take their cell phone, even to the grocery store, requires a mad dash home to retrieve it.

It is little wonder, then, that so many people (and not just Americans!) have no incentive or desire to learn about the roots of their so-called beliefs, even with a pervasive Internet. So, one could argue that *a left-leaning psychologically controlled environment continues on by default.* Fighting it simply requires too much work.

That means the opponents you are likely to encounter in meetings, forums, panels and committees won't necessarily be "the big guns." They may, however, have been *trained* by some "big guns." If an issue reaches a boiling point, or is expected to cause a furor, that's when "the big guns" are called upon for funds and "technical support." That's when, for example, the local teacher's union in Broken Arrow, Oklahoma, facing stiff opposition in a school board election, sent an S.O.S. to NEA's headquarters in the 1990s, which in turn sent representatives from one of its political arms like UniServ (mentioned previously). So, no matter how "local" you imagine an election to be, it isn't.

SECTION 4

Classic Adversarial Maneuvers

Attack manuals make use of "eavesdropper" (a.k.a. "snoop") surveys. Back in the early 1990s, the *Wall Street Journal* published such a survey on its editorial page—one that had been mailed to New York State Superintendents by the liberal-left New York Coalition for Democracy.

The Snoop Survey

The survey in question listed twenty-nine so-called "ultra-Right" organizations and asked survey recipients *whether they were aware of any materials or literature emanating from these sources.* Specific information was also requested concerning *how the recipient became aware* of "conservative" materials. Possibilities included supermarket flyers, voters' guides, letters to schools, and letters-to-the-editor. Red-flag terms included "conservative" expressions like *family values* and *dumb down.* So, the IRS was late to the party in screening for "conservative" red flag terms to target enemies of the liberal-left state in 2012–2013. This sort of thing had already been going on a long time.

The 1990s-era survey went on to ask whether there had been any known attempts to "censor, remove, or relocate" materials from school libraries, particularly out of concern for anti-religious or traditional sexual mores. Questions followed regarding any letter-writing campaigns, protests, or boycott threats by conservative groups relating to school speakers, plays, the arts, extracurricular programs, or exhibits.

Then, the capital offense: "Are there any faith-based churches [which] have endorsed school-board candidates or questioned the constitutional separation of church and state in your District? Please be specific."

The latter goes a step beyond older wording. By using the term "faith-based churches," rather than the smear "fundamentalist" or "Christian Right," the writers headed right for the jugular. The term "faith-based," for those who don't remember, was a hallmark of the George H. W. Bush administration. "Faith-based religion" was by the Clinton administration, a pariah, and faith itself was mocked.

The "snoop survey" is a typical tactic, and it is unfortunate that so many groups on the conservative side are either unable or unwilling to accumulate similar "human intelligence" on its adversaries. Thus, we are continually "preaching to the choir," still mostly stuck in the old mode of sending direct mail surveys to loyalists, all of them filled with questions skewed to elicit the predictable responses in hopes of soliciting funds. These fool no one, and irritate good allies.

Seeds of Doubt and Discontent

Washington State's version of the **NEA manual** (introduced earlier on: "What's Left After the Right?") has morphed from its 1986 origins to further advance a nationwide purpose: "to assist school personnel who have experienced, are experiencing, or who project they *will* experience, the conflict and trauma of a censorship controversy." This tactic is an appeal to fear, which we addressed earlier, as well as an attempt to sow seeds of doubt among any remaining educators who may still be harboring "conservative" or traditionalist views about teaching.

The key terms in the quotation above generate an *expectation of* "trauma." The manual implies that *all* schools can *expect* to be approached by loony parents who will throw an entire school system into turmoil. A sense of urgency is imparted.

Since the time of its printing, the text has been lengthened and refined by the NEA to allow cross-transfer value to other issues besides education. Where the State of Washington's version begins with a list of interchangeable smears used to describe the so-called enemies of education, later iterations have broadened subtitles such as "Background and Update on Censors vs. Public Education." Anyone who criticizes left-leaning NEA policies is portrayed as a censor—case closed—regardless of whether the policy relates to education, immigration, environment, foreign affairs or something else.

The point of the NEA's exercise in crafting attack manuals is, once again, to frame the debate in the reader's mind—to plant the idea that it is not merely "opponents" whom school personnel will be dealing with, but fanatics and "nut-cases."

So, when you show up at the school, or at any "concerned citizen" setting, there may already be a strike against you. Expecting hordes of fanatics to show up means that school staff are on alert—a position that is difficult for a smaller parent group to overcome.

Thinking "Clinically"

Of course, not everyone is going to be reached by your opponents; not everyone is going to "buy in." *Thus, your task, once again, is to reframe the debate and "plant seeds" of your own.* Take the advice of baseball professionals: "Keep your eye on the ball" (the goal); do not allow yourself to get caught up in the biases and diversions of opponents.

It's easier to keep a cool head if you focus on the technicalities of a question or issue instead of reacting to emotional "bait." Think clinically. Focus on the method, not the emotive language. Ask yourself repeatedly: What method is my opponent using against me? Eventually you will have to teach your children to do this too, or they will never be able to hold onto their values and opinions at the college level and beyond. For example, some version of a "Resident Assistant program" is alive and well in dormitories. Selected "residents" are tasked with reporting to university administrators any remarks and comments by students that reflect a conservative or traditionalist view. In fact, lawsuits have already been lodged against such programs on occasions when pupils are quick enough to pick up on what is happening and tell their parents.

Such was the case at the University of Delaware, which had launched an ideological reeducation program that was referred to in the university's own materials as a "treatment" for students' incorrect attitudes and beliefs—"a thorough thought-reform curriculum that was designed by the school's Residence Life staff in order to treat and correct the allegedly incorrect thoughts, attitudes, values, and beliefs of the students," according to Adam Kissel, the director of the Individual Rights Defense Program at the Foundation for Individual Rights in Education (FIRE), which handled the case and gave a speech on it in

2008. The "RA" program's stated goal was for the approximately seven thousand students in Delaware's residence halls to adopt highly specific university-approved views on politics, race, sexuality, sociology, moral philosophy, and environmentalism.

"Resident Assistant" programs like this one (under whatever name it shows up; the University of Delaware version was part of its Residence Life ("ResLife") program, whose operatives had been trained in confrontation techniques and was part of a newer "mandatory" indoctrination-programming model eerily similar to Adolf Hitler's.) exemplify why it is important to teach your children how to articulate their values and avoid getting caught up in "groupthink." Once the politically correct faction believes it has enough legitimacy to start reporting on and intimidating individuals who disagree with them, with a view to "shutting down" traditional moral and political attitudes out of fear for their job prospects upon graduation, then we have a situation reminiscent of the "Brownshirts" in Nazi Germany. As far back as 1998, FIRE founders Alan Charles, and Harvey A. Silverglate wrote a book entitled *The Shadow University: The Betrayal of Liberty on America's Campuses* (New York: The Free Press), stating: "Unknown to most faculty . . . a shadow university has emerged in offices whose mission used to be the delivery of services. Increasingly, offices of student life . . . have become agencies . . . whose mission is to bring students to mandatory political enlightenment."

Most people never read a thing about this important case. If they had, Americans everywhere would find it unsurprising when the leftist school union's **NEA manual** warns that "[a]nything outside the realm of the beliefs of the . . . Religious Right is considered anti-Christian, unpatriotic, demeaning to family tradition and undermines parental authority." Again, conservatives are characterized as inflexible, with an "absolutist mentality." Thus, our concept of "unchanging truths" is negatively construed; even though most people still believe that there are many timeless truths.

SECTION 5

Circumvention and Pre-Emption

On page 75 of the **NEA manual** is a questionnaire titled "Circumventing Censorship or Your Radical Right IQ." The respondent (usually someone seeking a position of leadership) is supposed to mark "yes," "no," or "don't know" beside each entry. This is an interesting "take" on the litmus test, as it will determine whether or not backing will be forthcoming from the educational establishment at election time. Among the more controversial survey items are these:

1. Has your district actively defined and promoted the concept of intellectual freedom for both the staff and community?
2. Is there an academic freedom policy or negotiated academic freedom clause in the teachers' contract?
3. Would you say, currently, that the vast majority of the teaching staff, administrators, and board of directors agree on a definition of academic freedom?
4. Has your district kept track of those community organizations who (*sic*) are most likely to be influenced by Far Right literature, speakers, tactics and pressure groups?

What can we glean from the four questions above?

ANSWER:

1. The survey items reveal how a respondent would handle (a) complaints from the community and (b) questions from the media. For example: Is he/she familiar with the buzz-terms?
2. Most questions revolve around an *ill-defined term.*

3. Resisters are *smeared* as not-very-bright, irrational censors.
4. The reader of the manual is surreptitiously being flattered.

If you figured these out already, move to the head of the class.

The most revealing suggestion from the manual is for school districts to set up a resource center or rolling "Far Right Cart"—no kidding! The purpose is to "make . . . censorship resources available to staff," complete with easy loan/check-out instructions!

Can you imagine what would happen if <u>conservative groups</u> set up a far-*Left* cart with politicized "tips" about handling provocation and hecklers?

As we move ever closer to the heart of litmus testing (should you be brave enough to run for school board or any other public office that impacts education), we see levels and sublevels of detail that reveal the education establishment's (especially the teachers union's) own biases, intentions and inflexibility. Let's look at a scenario the **NEA manual** sets out on page 110, concerning how to handle an incident of Right-Wing "censorship."

> **Situation:** A primary school library assistant (a mid-level school staffer) approaches a teacher, Board member, or Administrator about removing a set of books called Inner City Nursery Rhymes that contain profanity. The Board member looks through them and notices that they, in fact, <u>do contain</u> some profanity, AND IS OFFENDED, TOO. A check with the other elementary school across town reveals that it has the books also.

What to do?

Now for the zinger: ". . . [T]he assistant," states the manual, "belongs to the local Eagle Forum group."

That's enough, right there, to determine the strategy, because Eagle Forum is a nationally known conservative organization. Even though educators themselves may be offended by the books, *the manual advises that they not be removed, since doing so "implies permission for self-censorship to occur any time, by any person."* The advised seven-point response, under "Helpful Tips" (on page 112), is fairly typical of rebuttals by school officials to *any* complainant, be it staff or someone else:

- "Let complainants know you have heard their concern and that you will assist in every way possible to have the issue addressed . . . ." (*In other words, be polite and pretend you care*).
- "Refer to the district's policy and procedure for consideration of controversial materials." (**Procedure**, *otherwise known as "red tape," makes an excellent method for gaining both time and control. It wastes the complainant's time, frustrates and tires him out.*)
- "Explain that the concern must be submitted in writing." (*How many times have you heard that? More time-wasting—and you'd better be articulate.*)
- "Do not suggest that the book be removed. . . ." (*Translation: Don't give in until and unless the fire hits the fan.*)
- "Inform the building and central office administration, or whoever in the district has been designated as the one responsible for handling curricular-controversy issues." (*That is: Pass the buck and prolong the process.*)
- "Initiate the process for reconsideration . . . [b]ecause the book 'appears' . . . to be inappropriate, but ALWAYS follow the process." (*Translation: Cover your behind. Process over substance tends to solve all problems.*)
- Take time to re-familiarize yourself with the appropriate and related district policies. (*Translation: Look for loopholes.*)

So, let's condense all this into something usable. Here you have seven strategic points in the NEA's arsenal for handling controversy! You can boil them down to a more easily remembered, "translated" list:

1. Be polite and pretend to care.
2. Waste as much of the complainant's time as possible.
3. Maintain the upper hand and the psychological advantage.
4. Don't give in, even if you suspect the complainant is right because it sets a dangerous precedent.
5. Pass the buck and prolong the process.
6. Cover your "backside," and place process over substance.
7. Review and re-review policies for loopholes you can use.

Flipping over to a "Helpful Tips" section, the same publication suggest that any complainants be warned: "*[F]ree floating accusations will not be tolerated and legal action against them may be a consequence*"—an ironic threat, given that readers of the NEA manual have thus far endured some one hundred pages of "free-floating accusations," with no mention of "legal consequences." Somehow, writers missed the irony . . .

Under "Countering Far-Right Tactics," one finds additional guidelines:

- "Challenge the credibility of the attacking group. . . ."
- "Attempt to resolve confusion regarding misstatements, . . . clarify. . . ."
- "Avoid giving legitimacy . . . to Far Right charges. . . ."

These, too, can be reduced to something easily remembered and added these to the foregoing seven-point list:

8. Stereotype and label the opposition;
9. Promote the activity/curriculum, but <u>say</u> you're "clarifying the issue";
10. Marginalize the critics.

Now, let's bring out the **ASCD/ECS** attack **manual** (see the introduction to the Advanced Course for publication specifics). It carries four more ploys:

- Invite a group of critics to meet with you, listen attentively, then politely say that you will "take their comments 'under advisement' if common ground cannot be found"; and that your "job is to serve the greater good."
- If any "national experts" are being brought in by the group to talk to community members, find out who is paying for them to come, what interests they represent, and whether they represent the views of a vocal minority—then treat them accordingly.
- Make it clear to complainants, wherever possible, "that [the] community or state has decided that children should develop" whatever skills and abilities which the activity in question supposedly transmits.

So, let's summarize these, too, then add them to the ten-point list we have already compiled:

11. Pretend to take criticisms seriously by "taking them under advisement."

12. Always claim to be "serving the greater good"—i.e., the collective.
13. Marginalize any experts representing contrary views <u>prior</u> to their appearance. (Notice that your leftist opponents have long advocated finding out who, or what group, specifically, is funding or otherwise backing their side of the argument. Therefore, it behooves our side to do the same, as advised in Section 3 of the Beginner Course.
14. If possible, claim decisions are set by the state or other authorities.

Behold! In all, you now have 14 circumvention/brush-off tactics that will be used to sideline candidates whose political views are "fuzzy," parent complainants and for press relations. This is how the Left is going to "spin" education questions and contain criticism. View it as your adversaries' cache of attack-and-stall methods. Memorize them. Whatever argument may be used to rebuff your objections, on whatever grounds, you and/or your group can mentally refer to this list and decide <u>which</u> (and how many) of the 14 points are being activated. Be prepared to address them accordingly.

SECTION 6

Campaigns, Elections, and Outrageous Litmus Tests

Most attack manuals, including the NEA's, devote several pages to elections and campaigns, especially those related to school boards and local-regional regulators that get what is called "pass-through" money from state and federal government sources. In truth, most liberals and leftists would be just as happy to see local boards go away and all power transferred to federal or state education agencies. But since that is happening only sporadically (so far), considerable attention is devoted to local elections and campaigns, even where voting is minimal, to weed out "undesirables" before they can make a name for themselves.

Indeed, in the second paragraph of the section entitled "Participating in the School Board Election Process," the NEA manual, it states: "Every candidate for school board should be carefully interviewed by the education association and/or a patron committee early in the campaign regarding candidate views in educational issues."

Litmus Questions You Can Bank On

Notice the manual did **not** say *"interviewed by the community, parents, citizens, or taxpayers."* The only interview that <u>counts</u> is the one by "the education association" (that's the NEA and/or its state chapter and proxies). Where the manual alludes to "a patron committee," it means some proxy/puppet organization. The following list of questions serves as a series of short-answer litmus tests aimed at <u>weeding out</u> conservative candidates. Fail that, and you're in for a long haul. You will find that this is fairly typical of local elections not specifically connected with schools. State and locally elected office-seekers frequently use the same tactics, which is why, having this somewhere in writing is important. The following is quoted from the NEA manual:

- What are your top five objectives if elected to the school board?
- What is your view of the purpose of public education?
- How would you define the concept of academic freedom?
- How much latitude should the individual teacher have in his/her classroom?
- What is your view of the proper role of the school board and its members in relation to selection and retention of instructional materials?
- Do you have any specific changes you want to make in the curriculum offered in our district? If so, what and why?
- How would you respond to a parent who wants the district to limit access to or remove books from the library?
- Who should determine broad educational objectives? Specific course objectives?
- What limits, if any, would you like to see for employees teaching controversial issues?
- Who will you look to for advice on instructional matters?

Let's take these questions one at a time and identify the leftist-preferred answer so you can come up with a response that will help you instead of hurt you, without having to lie through your teeth:

1. *Do you have any specific changes you want to make in the curriculum offered in our district? If so, what and why?*
The NEA's preferred response will be that you would "like to strengthen academic freedom." (Naturally, you mean real, not phony, academic freedom, but leftist union leaders will probably not have an innocuous way to follow up on this response.)

2. *How would you respond to a parent who wants the district to limit access to or remove books from the library?*
The leftist-preferred response will basically be a reiteration of the first seven points "translated" (as per the previous section). Again,

worded this way, your leftist union adversaries will probably be at a loss to challenge you without coming across as biased:

- Be polite and caring.
- Buy time with procedures and paperwork.
- Maintain the upper hand and, therefore, the psychological advantage.
- Don't give in, even if you suspect the complainant is right.
- Consult a designated individual in the central office and prolong the process.
- Cover yourself.
- Place process over action.
- Review and re-review policies for loopholes you can use.

3. *"Should sex education be taught in the schools?"*

Anything but an enthusiastic affirmative on this question and your candidacy is dead. Therefore, say that you are for teaching about the human reproductive system, and that you would also like schools to spend additional time on the respiratory, digestive, nervous, circulatory and lymphatic systems so that students have a context in which to place sex.

4. *"How do you describe your position on separation of church and state?"*

Again, the NEA-preferred response is that any allusions to religious practice in schools are violations of the Constitution. Consequently, words to the effect that blatant establishment of a mandatory state religion was discouraged by the Founders. They had seen what happened with that approach in Europe. Ignore for the moment (at least in an opening statement) the fact that abridgment of the free exercise of religion was also not a function of government according to the founding documents. Leave this for later discussion. You do not want to give your adversaries an opening to discuss the "rights" of Wiccans, Islamic terrorists, and so on before you have firmly established your candidacy.

5. *"Where could the district spend less money? Where could it spend more?"*

Preferred answers will be somewhat locality-dependent, but in general, less emphasis on academic materials and more on school counselors, psychologists, gym equipment, and so on will pass the litmus test. So focus on the fact that since it is well-known that since it is well-known that American employers are looking for foreign students to fill technical and scientific slots because they are not finding them at home, your district doesn't want to be a newspaper advertisement for that trend. No one will argue with this response, because schools don't want negative publicity.

6. *"Do you believe more education dollars should go to early childhood education? Why or why not?"*

A hearty yes is expected, together with copious politically correct verbiage about getting kids "socialized." So focus your answer on "individual differences in readiness for school"—which technically addresses the early childhood question without giving specifics.

If you get past all these litmus-style questions, you can bet on additional hot-button, personal queries that separate the candidates who will, and will not secure leftist-NEA backing.

Long-Term Action Plans

All three attack manuals call for long-term action plans to create alliances, or partnerships, between educators and leftist organizations. They "run interference" for the education establishment <u>against</u> the public whenever necessary. The idea is that when trouble arises, there will be a certain familiarity, or loyalty, between liberal-leftist organizations and local policymakers to clear the path for a socialist agenda.

Our side does not have anything remotely approaching this level of organized resistance.

Our Side's Must-Do List

- A workable long-term strategy based on the litmus-test responses detailed above.
- Accomplished agents who can be called upon to "run interference" at local and regional levels.
- A slush fund for crises.
- Loyal patriots to serve as a buffer between targeted local candidates and the liberal/leftist super-organizations.

The following activities are already in progress by leftists according to their own literature. We must conduct parallel activities in the same way we once kept our <u>physical</u> defense systems equivalent to those of foreign enemies:

- Train our own cadre of experts and activists to serve as go-to people for panels, forums, and discussion groups.
- Conduct our own surveys and compile results to determine what we see as the *real* issues that need to be settled. This is incredibly expensive and should not be based in household-name, conservative think-tanks with the idea of getting predicable results and soliciting donations.
- Push real academic freedom and use the present window of opportunity to franchise private schools and set up online schools.
- Apply for grants with all sorts of friendly organizations and foundations to do exemplary projects that will provide viable alternatives to what the Left is offering. The Left is telling entities like state departments of education that with a little help from them, a statewide model will be provided that will "knock their socks off." The Left has secured a virtual monopoly on what is called the "pilot project," and we must respond in kind, right now!
- Establish a hot line where complaints and questions can be addressed quickly to counter the Left's "Rumor Stoppers."
- Hire full-time, high-powered public relations specialists that are friendly to our various causes.

Perception versus Reality

Now you have a glimpse into the extent of cooperation and funding that leftist organizations spend on ***molding public opinion***. Unhappily, the candidates our side fields tend to be a hodge-podge collection of average moms and pops and small, local txpayer groups having little or no financial backing or experience in hard-ball attack strategies like the ones above. Most simply "feel called upon" to run, which is admirable, but unfortunately inadequate. Occasionally these inexperienced candidates win, but their lives are made miserable in the process.

The essence of psychological warfare is what people <u>expect</u> you *will* do. It isn't about ideals, merit, track record or even reality. Those things show up <u>later</u>—after the game itself is virtually over.

Such is the essence of psychological warfare.

SECTION 7

How to Pursue Successful "Proactive" Counter-Measures

On page 16 of the **NEA manual**, readers learn in a side-note at the margin about another tactic favored by professional manipulators: "**[P]romote what we do rather than react to our critics** . . . ." In reality, this doesn't happen very often, as many of our lesser-trained adversaries get caught up in emotion the same as we do. If they get desperate, start ranting, and go into "attack mode," instead of staying focused on their mission, *that* can be good news for you. You can make use of such lapses, <u>provided you keep a "cool head."</u>

Leftists "Containment" Policies

The manual warns ominously that conservative parents tend to run for school board positions, to push for recall votes, serve on state and local committees, participate in telephone blitzes, lobby for legislation like home-schooling bills, file lawsuits, and volunteer as aides to get inside the classroom. These actions are called "proactive" measures—i.e., preemptive and practical. Even though the leftist organizations *do exactly the same things* described above, when traditionalists, constitutionalists and "conservatives" do them, these measures are treated as somehow *un*ethical, and which must be "contained."

What is an appropriate response?

Good comeback:

> "So what? Your side does all the same things—and with a lot more money behind you, too. The ACLU initiates frivolous lawsuits; the NEA subsidizes candidates for school board elections through its tax-exempt Uniserv unit. So, it's a draw. We both work to promote our people and our beliefs. Tell me something I don't know."

Angry denials (as in, "We do not do that!") are defensive and doomed. However, the "so what" comeback is <u>un</u>likely to be challenged.

One interesting fact the writer of the **NEA manual** let slip was that some 30 percent of the resistance comes to school programs and policies from <u>school staff</u>, including teachers. This says a lot about just how disgruntled the foot-soldiers of the profession itself are, despite the NEA's public relations to the contrary. Our side needs to capitalize on that, because all teachers, principals and administrators are *not* happy with the leftist agenda in education.

Perfect Timing

Thankfully, technology has handed us more than spam and identity theft. It has offered us a unique opportunity, beginning in earnest only since about 2010, to pull the rug out from under the leftist education establishment in a truly proactive way. Online courses of study—even entire elementary, secondary, and specialized university-level curricula—are now being offered through the Internet. For years, establishment educators and the teachers unions have worked to demonize and marginalize home-schools, private education options (unless they are very liberal and incorporate leftist curriculum choices), and religious schools. Catholic schools, for example, had the foresight early on to virtually franchise themselves nationwide, which is one reason the Catholic Church has undergone an unmerciful bashing over the few years. Catholic education is a bit less expensive than other private school options, as it is partially subsidized by the enormous resources of the Catholic Church; consequently, many parents, Catholic or not, have pulled their children from increasingly dangerous and ineffective public schools and pursued the Catholic education route.

But a few of these schools, like individual Catholic parishes, connect with the Left; others are still traditionalist in their conduct expectations and offer strictly academic curricula. Either way, the capability to franchise endlessly makes Catholic schools a threat to establishment educators and union leaders who prefer a government system that is rigorous only in its political indoctrination and culture-rot-laden environment. Again, government accomplishes this with bait-and-switch schemes and other offers of "free money"—always in the name of some "good cause."

Because conservative groups have failed to massively franchise a traditionalist, constitutionalist and patriotic system of schools (one or two here and there are not enough), we have virtually lost the education battle and sacrificed nearly two generations of youngsters to leftist-socialism.

All that can now change, despite the Left's effort to deny accreditation to home schools and private schools it doesn't like. Those who would save our way of life and re-establish the American Dream have a short window of opportunity to inundate the nation—and indeed the free world—with online options. Given the uptick in school violence and bullying, the tables could literally be turned against the Left. Such a proactive move would also be profitable, and given the number of Internet users now—just look at the number of Facebook and other social networking users—j it still requires too much in the way of staff and budget for individual states, or college entrance officials, to deny accreditation to *all* online schools.

One thing could change that—which is why this is a **short** window of opportunity: control of the Internet by government. As nearly everyone is aware, our federal government, and even world bodies like the United Nations, are trying every underhanded method their leftist elites can think of to regulate, tax or otherwise intrude upon the use of the Internet. So far, privacy advocates and other groups have kept these elites at bay. However, once government gets its fingers in the Internet door, the game changes.

That is why it is critical to saturate the Internet with a variety of online school options. It is okay if some online schools offer a "progressive" curriculum, because some parents want that. Remember, the element of surprise is critical to success. Yes, you want education to be more traditional, but you also want all parents to have options. We do not have that under the current, stacked-deck system. We must brainstorm into existence a new system. That system is online education. Then parents and students can avail themselves of whichever type of study they want.

As the famous line from the movie, *Field of Dreams*, goes: "If you build it, they will come." If enough people buy into the concept of Internet schooling, then, like the cell phone, nothing can truly stop its spread.

The **NEA manual** instructs its left-leaning educators to *sell the advantages of an offending curriculum, project, activity or text—to promote it,* instead of addressing any of the complainant's concerns. Why do they advise this? Because it reflects an offensive strategy, not a defensive one. Again, our side should take notice, not because we want to offend anyone, but because we have something of worth to disseminate, and at some profit, too (for a change).

Moreover, it is not a question of "growing" the conservative tent by "being more inclusive"—i.e., by throwing in the towel and rethinking key constitutional and moral principles, something several Republican leaders have suggested since the defeat of Mitt Romney and many congressional candidates in the 2012 election. It is not accomplished by shutting down the government, as in October 1, 2013—which does nothing more than "create the conditions" for another Democratic election sweep. (If you have to ask "why," go back to the Principles of Psych-War: a gigantic, left-leaning bureaucracy will still get paid and remain in place. Only the most irritating and least-expensive federal and state programs will be shut down temporarily, such as the National Zoo.) This is the essence of a "containment" strategy, only the Left is using it instead of our side! It is a question of inaugurating original services, coming up with something that people want that also happens to reflect our beliefs, and promoting it in locations where the Left believes it has already secured the edge—as in education.

Other Viable, Proactive Strategies

There's simply no excuse for conservatives to be endlessly complaining about the media or, say, illegal aliens unless they intend to mount a serious, no-holds-barred campaign to put their money where their mouth is, and do it with outside-the-box thinking.

For example, conservatives and traditionalists need to flood the entire culture with interesting entertainment venues. There is no need to refer to such efforts in terms that are bound to raise the hackles of leftists even before they are aired, read, or heard (terms like "family friendly," for instance, have already been marginalized; so find another expression). The Left understood how to "contain" us long ago, and that, essentially, is how they beat us. It is up to us, now, to come up with our own buzz-terms, slogans, promotions and materials. We should act as though the leftist opposition is no more than an irritating mosquito (which is how the Left treats traditionalists), instead of doing them the service of announcing that we are going to counter something the Left does, in effect reciting their own slogans back to them, such as "diversity programs," causing the public to fixate on the Left's slogan instead of on what we are offering!

Who concocted the term "diversity"? You? Conservatives? Traditionalists? No, the Left did. Who turned it into a household name-brand? Not conservatives—knowingly, anyway. So why do we keep repeating this expression? To do so is to gobble the opposition's bait! Similarly, we need to reset the debate over race and ethnicity by improvising something else.

Now consider the issue of generating a new line of TV dramas and comedies, plays, songs, films and news services that is not endlessly imbued with blood, vomit, foul language, demeaning put-downs and death. It's not as if we need to hunt around for a potential audience! We already *have* an audience—more than we think!

Real talents, with broad appeal, fill stadium-sized auditoriums (due mostly to word of mouth and public television), yet they rarely get an airing on mainstream radio and TV—stand-out singers like Josh Grobin, Susan Boyle, Mark Vincent, Andrea Bocelli, Sarah Brightman, Karen Akers, Audra McDonald, Patti LaPone and too many instrumentalists to list. Why are these true talents not being supported financially by "conservative" benefactors? On the other hand, individuals who can barely carry a tune and whose acts resemble the antics of hookers and pimps—among them, Beyoncé, Britney Spears, Paris Hilton, and Christina Aguilera and the late Michael Jackson—have been showered with media intention and funding.

The Left changed the rules of the game in the 1960s, by underwriting first, real talent that leaned leftward and saw an opportunity in popularizing songs and shows that, although left-leaning, were nevertheless of high quality. Having achieved their goal of establishing certain attitudes in the public mind, especially teenagers, the Left suddenly switched gears and began subsidizing smut and gore. The musicality of Joan Baez and the Kingston Trio and the mostly good, clean fun of sitcoms like "Sanford & Son," "Happy Days," and "Barney Miller" disappeared, and were replaced with tuneless, talentless excuses-for-artists like the Beastie Boys and Eminem, not to mention the dubious merriment of bathroom humor and contrived "contests." The envelope has been pushed even further with the opening of 2014 season that began in September 2013.

This game can be changed. Whereas entertainment once served to refresh the psyche and induce relaxation, as well as to enthrall and appeal to our sense of adventure, it mostly devolved into whatever was horrifying, uncomfortable and emotionally crushing. An occasional foray into issues that give one pause and make us think is one thing; a non-stop, communal death wish is another.

What traditionalists and people of taste must do is locate and enlist, on a massive scale, with the aid of benefactors and organizations that will help advance the careers of high-grade talents. We need to scout out and hire producers, screen writers, song writers and performers whose work is uplifting and who can create material that appeals to people *other than* hard-core leftists and delinquents.

You may, or may not, support *federal* funding for the Corporation for Public Broadcasting. No matter: Let's give the Public Broadcasting Service (PBS) its due. It has long succeeded in providing real, "adult"-appealing material; for example, when it aired programs like "Yes, Minister" and "All Creatures Great and Small" in the 1980s, "Rumpole of the Bailey," in the 1990s; and "Foyle's War" in the 2000s, and whenever it introduces audiences to groups like Rolling Thunder, Three Tenors and Celtic Woman. Only a lack of general advertising for these shows and talents initially reduced audience share, but thousands of Americans found the shows anyway. You may have been one of them, and wondered why you didn't see them advertised more often or picked up by other new networks.

Dramatic series like "Foyle's War" and "Yes, Minister," garnered enormous viewerships. In fact, it would have been difficult or impossible to replace a single major actor or actress in these series; they were that good! The lines themselves were difficult enough even for a seasoned actor to pull off, especially in the case of "Yes, Minister" and its sequel, "Yes, Prime Minister." All these shows are still re-aired, and are sold as DVD sets, too.

Worthy dramas and comedies absolutely *will* garner a large following, but conservatives have to be willing to invest their time and money. Hundreds of producers and screen writers are yearning for an opportunity to show what they can do, and they frequently hit a home run when they get it. *Let's divert the enormous sums we waste on politicians and political action/campaign committees into <u>saturating</u> the culture via the air-waves. What good is a candidate, if nearly the entire mass media is busy disparaging America's views 24/7?* If conservatives can't slow the flow of culture rot into America's living rooms; if we can't at least get someone who can actually sing the National Anthem to perform for the Superbowl; if we can't insist on real journalism instead of "infotainment," then (as the expression goes), we "got nothin'!"

Proactive Problem-Solving

In keeping with the concept of proactive (as opposed to <u>re</u>active) thinking, traditionalists and constitutionalists need to come up with unique ways of solving national issues, particularly if it is a controversial problem that is weighing heavily on the public mind.

It doesn't matter whether the reason for the public's deep concern has been "planted" by the leftist media or by a sitting administration. Perhaps the issue in question legitimately emanates from the citizenry itself. Whatever the case, at this juncture in the nation's headlong dive toward socialism, those who call themselves "real conservatives" must start putting bandages on problems and initiate original, understandable, and hard-hitting breakthroughs that capture the attention of a majority of the populace.

Never mind whether your target audience on a particular issue votes or doesn't vote; whether it is "liberal" or "conservative"; whether it is among the "47 percent" that pays no taxes, or is employed. The viewer or reader may be wealthy or live paycheck-to-paycheck. The point is to capture his attention.

Let's take, for example, immigration.

Both liberals and conservatives are making this issue inordinately difficult. Everything currently "on the table" is seen by the public either as a nod to amnesty for illegals (especially criminals), or as grossly unfair to individuals who have worked hard, earned their keep and have come to this country to succeed in a way they could not in their native land—just like many of our forebears. Whether legislators or the sitting administration calls its proposed legislation a "pathway to citizenship," a "compromise position," or just a "realistic approach," most Americans aren't buying it. Everything politicians come up with is either too complicated or controversial. Nothing but protests from one side or the other have been generated. The current climate is not a winner for either side.

So, why not try an up-front approach to the immigration debate? Whatever we come up with on this topic, of course, must take into consideration the pervasive threat of foreign terrorism from sleeper cells and individuals who overstay their visas. Thus, it makes sense (and is honest) to place a *temporary moratorium* on all immigration until the US has a game plan—until, as the saying goes, "we get our act together." We need to buy time to put in place new rules of the game, and we can't do that as things stand.

If we go the "temporary moratorium" route, it should extend to asylum-seekers; otherwise, there emerges exception after exception, until we are back where we started—with wave upon wave of newcomers for whom there can be no means of accounting. So, we could start off by closing our doors to newcomers, but only until we figure out what to do about the millions of illegal immigrants who are already here (there are far too many now to deport), and until we establish an intake procedure that works *at least* as well as the old Ellis Island.

A sponsorship policy for new arrivals once was workable, and might be worth considering again, with a little tweaking of that system to accommodate the easy travel options that exist today.

Either a newcomer has a sponsor who is a US citizen with *no* criminal record, or doesn't. That is something verifiable, whether the foreigner in question is on a student visa or has any one of several types of work visas.

Immigration laws once protected native and naturalized US citizens, by denying visas and applications for citizenship to anyone presenting a clear and present danger to residents of this country *or to his/her own native country.* The United States could refine and narrow the old no-admittance list to individuals who:

- have a communicable disease (all applicants are subject to a physical examination by a qualified physician);
- have committed a serious criminal act(s) in his/her home country (all applicants are subject to a background check that is at least as rigorous as American citizens who require a job-related Top Secret clearance here at home);
- are known terrorists, have been (or are currently) members of a politically subversive group in their home country or in other countries

(this is <u>not</u> the same as political profiling of <u>current</u> US citizens, as applicants are *seeking* entry or applying for residency as *non*-citizens);

- are members of a faction or elite corps that is hostile to the United States (such as Iran or Somalia), or who either currently is or has been convicted as a war criminal (whether the conviction was fair cannot be weighed in the current climate of terrorism, so we should err on the side of the conviction standing).
- have used illegal means to enter the United States within the past five years. (If this is the *only* negative that is relevant to an application-denied decision, then the "five years" caveat allows for some compromise. If, however, an illegal means of entry occurs in combination with any *other* of the items on the list, then illegal entry would carry additional weight in the application process).

The uncovering of terrorist cells inhabited by relatively recent immigrants-turned-citizens and persons who overstayed their visas in several US cities, not to the mention mass-terror attacks in London, Madrid and Boston, cries out for a sixth layer of protection, if we are to maintain what remains of Americans' dwindling respect for the Constitution, state laws and the police.

For example, Boston Marathon bombing suspects, brothers Dzhokhar and Tamerlan Tsarnaev, somehow managed to remain in the United States legally for some eleven years, under asylum, with citizenship papers pending before the attack, even though they hailed from renowned cesspools of violence and fanaticism: Chechnya and neighboring Dagestan. Practically the entire Tsarnaev family received welfare benefits and subsidies of one kind or another for years, compliments of US taxpayers, even with the brothers, particularly Dzhokhar's, ongoing ties to radical ideologues in their native country, some of whom may have helped train them in bomb-making. It is not at all unusual for immigrants from hostile countries to avail themselves of welfare benefits once on US soil.

Thus, the addition of a sixth, and final, requirement for prospective immigrants—sponsorship that carries a meaningful set of obligations:

- The applicant has a sponsor in the United States who is a US citizen in good standing, with no criminal background or history of violence. The sponsor pledges to take responsibility for the applicant's status, either as a *bona fide* refugee (i.e., applicant is granted asylum by appropriate government authorities); as a guest worker; as a foreign student on temporary visa; or as an individual seeking permanent citizenship and residence in the United States. Said sponsor provides regular verification that the applicant is gainfully employed by a legitimate establishment or proprietor legally headquartered within the United States, or that the applicant is on the roster as a student and signed up for/attending at least four classes during his/her stay. The sponsor assures the US government that the applicant's children, present or future, who *reside with applicant for the duration of his/her stay* (or until permanent US citizenship is secured) all have health care, day care or attend educational facilities that do *not* entail taxpayer dependency. Sponsor shall bear responsibility for any violent or criminal acts committed, or tied to, the applicant (as established in a court of law) for a period of up to fifteen years, which constitutes the maximum time period allowed temporary residents.

Now, such obligations of sponsorship as described above may, or may not, reflect all that we wish to incorporate into a citizenship application. The above argument may, or may not, comprise a solution to illegal immigration. That is not the point of the foregoing exercise. The point is that the draft above is (a) rational, (b) comprehensible, (c) concise, (d) memorable and (e) reflective of the current era. It is proactive.

Unless traditionalists, constitutionalists and all those wishing to call themselves "conservatives," are willing to take the time to tailor and advance a proposal along specific lines, such as the one proposed above on the immigration debate, they have *no business tossing insults at those who do*. We either set the agenda and dictate the terms of debate, or continue to allow the Left to control psychological environment, to hijack entire topics and issues, to disrupt our alliances, and to keep us running about helter-skelter, as outlined in the Rules of Psych War.

The above sponsorship provision would greatly reduce the options of "unaffiliated" or "unknown" terrorists working to set up shop in the United States, complete with visas and/or questionable citizenship papers, then biding their time and even recruiting others for nefarious purposes.

"POST-GRAD" COURSE—ROOTS OF MANIPULATION

Introduction

For those of you who are really "hooked" at this point on the subject of manipulation and are interested in its origins and how it "morphed" behind the scenes, you may find it helpful peruse a short backgrounder. You probably are particularly curious as to how this wound up in the United States, proliferating in a constitutional democracy that prides itself on certain individual rights.

The short answer, of course, is that the sophistication of manipulative strategies described in the forgoing pages did not originate here, although it is within the nature of some people in every country to crave control over others. Consequently, there is always a willing audience for this sort of thing. Some professions tend to attract control freaks—in this country, what are called the behavioral sciences seem to entice such persons, and politics is a draw in any country—so it is not surprising to find niches lodged within these fields. Because educators and marketing/public relations degree programs are increasingly filled with behavioral science courses, it figures that individuals exposed continually to manipulation strategies are going to absorb some of the conditioning techniques.

SECTION 1

Psy-Ops: The Threads, the Glue, and the Means

There are four <u>threads</u> that run though what is known in intelligence circles as "psy-ops" (psychological operations) programs, which are associated with all forms of high-level manipulation. Then, there is the proverbial <u>glue</u> that holds them all together.

The monikers typically associated with hard-ball strategies include the Delphi Technique, the Alinsky Method, Group Dynamics, the Tavistock Method and one other, which inadvertently made its way into the news relatively recently, *perception management (PM)*. The latter term comes to us compliments of the US Defense Department. *Perception management* is characterized by the Defense Department's own website as "actions to convey and/or deny selected information. . ., to influence . . . emotions, motives, and objective reasoning . . . ultimately resulting in foreign behaviors and official actions favorable to the originator's objectives. . . ." "[PM] combines truth projection, operations security, cover and deception, and psychological operations."

The Wikipedia definition of PM adds: the "imposition of falsehoods and deceptions [to get] the other side to believe what one wishes it to believe."

So, let's move on to two important subsets common to all five major monikers above—Delphi, Alinsky, Group Dynamics, Tavistock and PM. These are *sensitivity training* (a.k.a. "T-Groups" and "encounter sessions") and *re-education* (a term that stuck following discovery of the infamous "re-education camps" in North Korea, the old Soviet Union, and Maoist China). The threads that run through both subsets are:

- intimidation
- semantic deception

- conditioning
- programming (a.k.a., "brainwashing")

The glue that holds the threads together is marketed to unsophisticated readers of the daily news as *political enlightenment*, usually worded as "today's enlightened age." To collegiates, corporate executives, and heads of important bureaus and offices it is called *behavior modification*. The latter used to have at least some ignominy attached to it, but now "behavior mod" has become popularized.

But to intelligence professionals, the "glue," whether it's called political enlightenment or behavior modification, boils down to just one thing: *scientific coercion*. If some scandal emerges, and they need a euphemism for press or public relations purposes, they may call it "information warfare," or the more benign-sounding "molding public opinion." So, what you have here is words aimed at redefining, or obfuscating, other words that people might find objectionable. For that reason, we must get a handle on all this by defining each of the four threads in the bulleted list above.

Intimidation, of course, is a common term, and in the present context means tarnishing a person's (or an organization's) reputation, status, credibility and/or line of business.

Semantic deception involves the misleading use of words, as with the term "political enlightenment" for the more accurate (but offensive) term, "behavior modification." Another example is using the term "community organizer" instead of the more accurate designations "professional agitator" or "provocateur." "Humanizing education" is probably an obvious euphemism by now to the readers of this section. "Leveling the playing field," substituted for an artificial imposition of equal outcomes for all, is a little harder to spot.

As for the other two "threads," the question always comes up as to whether it is correct to use the words "conditioning," "brainwashing" and "programming" interchangeably. Not exactly, no; but for practical purposes, yes: All involve repetition using various formats. *Conditioning* involves reward-and-punishment (in the manner of Ivan Pavlov's salivating dog), and tends to be less harsh and more easily pulled off than either programming or brainwashing. The "punishment" in the use of conditioning as a technique of individual or group manipulation is typically not corporeal, but more along the lines of ridicule, ostracism or loss of status.

"Brainwashing," strictly speaking, tends to utilize a one-on-one, hard-hitting approach involving deprivation and non-lethal, emotional torture, whereas "programming" can be applied to larger groups that share a cause. Sometimes "programming" is targeted to a particular demographic, especially one that is known to have unique needs (such as teenagers and retirees).

What all these techniques *do* have in common, however, is that they set a person up for an emotional (psychological) fall. Professional agitators and provocateurs play with the unsuspecting victim's mind, say by pitting perceived "authorities" against each other, or by inducing anguish, guilt or remorse. The purpose is always to shut down rationality.

Whether one is talking about the Delphi Technique, Saul Alinksy's "Rules for Radicals," Kurt Lewin's "Group Dynamics," the National Training Lab's encounter tactics, or John Rawlings Rees' Tavistock Method of inducing mass neurosis (i.e., obsession, fixation or phobia), all the strategies have been refined and adapted over the years since about 1935 by various entities (for example, educators, "community activists," protest organizers, etc). These entities, therefore, may no longer be directly associated with the originators, who have died and left a cadre of disciples to carry on. Many of these disciples added their own twist to the basic strategies.

Which brings us to the core strategies themselves, among them:

- instituting some form <u>disruption/disorganization</u>: imposition of chaotic interruptions that compromise the train of thought and the sequencing of ideas, so that actions and opinions wind up appearing irrational and impulsive.
- generating <u>cognitive dissonance</u> (a.k.a. "the Catch-22"): pressure to believe, or accept, two diametrically opposing ideas at the same time.
- <u>desensitizing</u> the public or group: acclimating individuals to that which is ugly or abhorrent until at last the behavior or concept is seen as "no big deal."
- using <u>negative and positive reinforcement</u>: use of psychologist B. F. Skinner's reward and punishment scheme, as per his classic "operant conditioning."
- ensuring <u>involuntary attention</u>: use of interdisciplinary formats and surreptitious presentations that incorporate values and ideas that nobody can avoid viewing or hearing repeatedly.

- encouraging <u>self-disclosure:</u> self-reports which are potentially embarrassing.
- popularizing the concept of <u>social control</u>: for example, the TSA uses "threat of terrorism" to force a ninety-year-old in a wheelchair to remove her soiled, adult diaper, and people may swallow their angst, but somehow find that acceptable.
- applying some kind of <u>social stimulus</u>: for example, because media attention tends to make one an overnight sensation, one form of stimulus is to place a recognized TV or cable-channel network truck with reporters and cameras at a scene.
- instituting <u>encounter sessions</u>: forcing people to undergo hypothetical situations where they are screamed at and verbally abused by the group.
- engaging the person in <u>sociometrics</u>: This is a key aspect of <u>group dynamics</u> used to sow sowing frustration, distrust, anger, envy, emotional pain, and even despair.
- superimposing a new (or previously stigmatized) <u>value structure</u>: supplanting one value with another by constantly adding "exceptions."
- establishing <u>psychological threshold</u>: This indicates a point at which most subjects can be expected to "break," or "crack."
- stripping out the existing <u>belief system</u>: removing or calling into question a person's emotional support system.
- <u>internalizing</u>, or normalizing, new beliefs: overwhelming the rational belief system so that the new "value" or idea becomes second nature.
- encouraging <u>behavioral reversion</u>: lapse or relapse into an earlier behavior so that the conduct is uncharacteristic of the individual's current situation or age, as in a forty-year-old suddenly sucking his/her thumb; or instilling a mob mentality so that the demands of the group overwhelm some normal individual inhibition, such as running naked in a crowded street.

The terms underlined in the above list can be found in any dictionary of psychology or psychiatry. Books and articles about each one can be easily referenced. As the reader no doubt has surmised, the foregoing provides a jaw-dropping view concerning the roots of opinion-molding and mind-manipulation.

The preceding list also serves to reinforce a point, alluded to earlier on: that *mind* and *brain* are not synonymous. No tactic on this list, regardless of how rigorously applied, actually damages the brain as an organ of the body. The brain, *per se,* remains intact; no medical test could prove organ damage, with the possible exception of a tangential rise in blood pressure, which usually accompanies stress.

The *mind*, on the other hand, *is* affected—unless the individual recognizes s/he is under siege, is able to process what is happening, can *intellectualize* it (i.e., substitute rationality for emotionality); and realizes that, physiologically, the tormenter cannot do actual harm unless the victim allows it. But, of course, this is very difficult to achieve in real time.

Nevertheless, virtually all talk-style therapy is built around the above tenet: Nobody can torment another person mentally without his/her emotional consent. *What makes one vulnerable is that everybody has feelings and a personality.*

As indicated previously, sometimes one is not in a position to withhold mental consent, as in the case of children who are, from a legal standpoint, part of a *captive audience* in their classrooms. Still, from a *clinical* standpoint, anyone who is firm or confident in his/her beliefs is not likely to be moved—unless one other kind of pressure is applied: psychiatric drugs. This introduces a whole new dimension to the game and *can* definitely affect the brain as an organ, in which case the mind is affected, too, as it resides (so to speak) inside the brain.

Because psychiatric drugs haven't been around long enough to predict long-term effects with any degree of certainty, placing still-growing, maturing youngsters on such drugs for reasons related to irritating habits, high-energy levels, temper tantrums, forgetfulness, fidgeting, and not paying attention is highly dangerous to both the child and society.

A Cautionary Note on Health-Care Opportunists

Let's face it, whether you're talking about the brain as an organ, or the mind and how thought works, the foregoing discussion makes for some fascinating topics. It's not hard to see why bright individuals get caught up in mind games and wish to make some aspect of manipulation into a career. If one is upset enough, common sense dictates that the resulting stress can make you physically sick, and even forgetful or irritable on a long-term basis—which is never a good deal for the sufferer. It is this fact which blurs the lines between psychology and physiology, or mind and body, and as with everything else, there are always opportunists around to exploit these lines.

For this reason, a cautionary note is appropriate here: Do not assume that either clinical or experimental psychology is wholly bogus—or necessarily banal. While the field of behavioral psychology and the mental "health" industry tend to get a bad rap in these pages, do not underestimate its chief practitioners' capabilities.

While it is true that the field hasn't figured out enough to do people much good—that is to say, they can't "cure" depression, phobias, obsessions, or any of the various "disorders" (fictitious or otherwise) listed in the *Diagnostic and Statistical Manual of Mental Disorders* (DSM)— the bible of the profession—those who specialize in these areas *have* been able to identify and categorize tendencies and quirks of personality that appear to go hand-in-hand. Unfortunately, opportunists have gone on to exploit vulnerable individuals and groups who share similar attitudes, worldviews and penchants. We explored some of these in Section 1 of the Beginner Course, under Consensus and so-called "Preventative Psychiatry"—with individuals like Chris Mooney, Robert McCrae, Arie Kruglanski, Robert Altemeyer, and others whose politicized "studies" were the products of government and university grants.

Fortunately, there are other truly honest and dedicated specialists who have dedicated their lives to helping troubled individuals who seek their services without politicizing their work or pushing psychotropic "cocktails" to their patients. What they try to do, instead, is to help their patients brainstorm approaches to sorting out problems in a way that is in keeping with their personalities. Because they come at the problem as "outsiders" or "spectators,"—that is to say, someone not so close to the situation as the patient—these students of the mind can stand back, as it were, and view their patients' circumstances from a neutral position. These specialists understand the limitations of their field. A principled specialist of this type will invariably refer the patient to a medical doctor to rule out physiological health issues. For example, allergies (especially the unusual ones) *can* affect the brain as an organ and wreak havoc; it may take extensive tests—a sort of process-by-elimination, which can be both lengthy and exhausting—but eventually it *will* show up in a genuine medical test in fluids, blood or on X-ray.

Unfortunately, there is a significant cabal of *un*principled mental-health specialists, too. Always remember that the umbrella term for psychology, psychiatry, sociology, psychotherapy, and related fields is "behavioral science." As with medical science, some careerists end up on the clinical side, some on the experimental side, and some as practitioners.

It is the faction of "behavioral science" that believes society can be improved for the better—and for political gain—by changing people's belief systems on a mass scale, as well as on individual scale, that concerns us here. This cabal, or faction, is the one that is targeting teacher education, K–12 classrooms, university administrations, workplaces, houses of worship and even the bureaucracy via mandatory "workshops" and lectures. The invasiveness of this faction is made worse by the quantum leap in technological capability over the past thirty years; it is aided and abetted by sophisticated computer equipment that collects, stores, cross-matches and shares data in a way that would have made Hitler and Stalin drool with envy.

The particular cabal we are talking about here is almost exclusively left-leaning. Its primary tenet is that traditional concepts about "morality," "decency," "shame," and right and wrong are not only vastly overrated but unhealthy.

Take the concept of guilt. According to this elite circle within the the field of behavioral science, "guilt" produces neurosis, which is to say, it makes us sick and therefore should be expunged as a credible concept. The same goes for any moral "absolute." They justify their view by point-ing out that there are always "situations" and "circumstances" that, in ef-fect, change the playing field. But this view contains two of the fallacies we examined in the Intermediate Course: the **hasty generalization** and the **false hypothesis:** Just because there are sometimes extraordinary circumstances that override normal judgment, *therefore* they believe the entire baby—i.e., the concept of guilt or shame or right and wrong—should be eradicated across-the-board.

Indeed, the World Federation for Mental Health, among other entities, subscribes to this notion. According to one of its founders and most eminent leaders, the late Dr. G. Brock Chisholm, it is up to psychiatrists to cure our society by eliminating traditional—and supposedly erroneous—concepts about right and wrong! The result was called "situational ethics," which is today the New Morality.

A smörgåsbord of practicing specialists championing this view were cited in Section 2 of the Beginner Course; others include Drs. Chester M. Pierce, Ewen Cameron, and John Rawlings Rees (whom we will "meet" in a few pages). And who could forget good old Sigmund Freud? These men and their disciples and colleagues conspired with well-connected educational theorists like Edward Thorndike and Benjamin Bloom to "program" an entire generation of teachers and school administrators into the New Morality (a.k.a. "human potential movement" and "self-actualization movement"), which by the 1970s had become thoroughly embedded in education policymaking at the highest levels. Their views on the fallibility of right and wrong can be easily accessed online and in professional periodicals (start with http://www.psychquotes.com/ and take it further from there). Since the reader can easily verify this intention to fundamentally change society in the post-World War II era by accessing statements and writings of these men and their colleagues, there is no need to provide lengthy quotations here to prove the point. This faction of behaviorists has long been vocal about its dogma and its intention to reframe society—generously appropriating the taxpayer's dime to accomplish it.

Today, the crusade against old ("bourgeois"?) ideas of right and wrong and what used to be called "public decency" is pervasive. Just turn on the TV or an ordinary radio station. The original theorists created a tentacled web that is both influential and well-funded, organizations whose leaders and followers continue to operate under the misguided assumption that they are either "saving humanity" or that there will be something in it for them, financially (e.g., psychopharmaceutical drugs) or politically (e.g., places of leadership and status on important panels connected with the United Nations, the World Federation of Mental Health, and other worldwide bureaucracies and NGOs). As from time immemorial, opportunists find the thought of control over large swathes of the population incredibly seductive.

In any case, this faction's theorists and promulgators, such as those mentioned above, both living and deceased, remain remarkably absent from high school and college textbooks. But they effectively cost America the Cold War and set the stage for our nation's present violence-laden and sex-saturated environment. Foreign terrorists are merely "the cherry" on the proverbial sundae.

The Roots of Forced Choices

It is helpful here to revisit the whole business about mind-versus-brain. One of the more cogent explanations concerning the difference comes from the late Emmet Fox, reiterated many times in his books and speeches on theology and philosophy during the 1930s and '40s. He was particularly struck by the fact that no action—nothing that one actually sees, either in a town or city, or for that matter in the universe—can occur which is not preceded by a thought. Try, if you can, to picture a state of mind—e.g., fear, sorrow, envy, sensuality or virtues like compassion—as a material object. You can't do it. Only a representation, or picture— say, of a human being expressing terror on his face, or a film depicting the victims of an earthquake or hurricane, in tears or aguish, can be depicted. So concepts like fear, justice, remorse, and jealousy are abstract qualities that cannot, *by themselves,* be held in one's hand.

What professional manipulators do is evoke these abstract qualities in you, draw them out, *force* you to express them. The more sensitive the person, the easier the job. The manipulator cannot hand any of these emotions to you, nor can they assail your actual brain (without using drugs or other physical means). What the manipulator **wants** is to tap into your unconscious yearnings, desires, dislikes and so on—the belief system you have built up so far, and of which you are unaware— and distort what is there so that you will think differently, and more importantly, **react** differently than you would have, had you been left to your own devices. To accomplish that, the manipulator must first know what your yearnings, desires and dislikes *are*—which means surveys, questionnaires and other data collection.

Schools, of course, use make wide use of surveys and questionnaires. Pupils do not put their names on them and assume, therefore, they are "anonymous." But a bar code, embedded-label or identifier is usually on the response form (online and/or on paper), and if someone should ask, such as a parent, s/he is told that the information is "confidential." In a legal context, "confidential" means "need to know." Who needs to know? Maybe school administrators, college entrance officials, the FBI (especially if you ever need a security clearance), Child Protective Services agencies, various employers. It makes no difference that such information can be encrypted and sent electronically.

Such tools combined with cross-matched information from, say, magazine subscriptions, favorite vacation spots, political party preference, religious affiliation, and so on—any of which, today, is easily accessed via computer—makes prediction that much easier and simplifies the task of "getting inside your head."

SECTION 2

The "Negative Trigger" Effect

As indicated earlier on, both young children and adolescents, including college-age students are particularly susceptible to emotional manipulation, especially if caught up in a "captive environment" situation. That is the root of the familiar saying that "children are vulnerable," and more easily traumatized by events.

Youth, combined with a lack of real-world experience, make it easy to misinterpret events. This is understandable, as toddlers, pre-teens and teenagers have a tougher time recalling details, much less intellectually processing (instead of merely reacting to) events and formulating some plan to deal with their tormenters.

This is the biggest reason why it is imperative that caring, responsible (adult) parents raise children, not professional babysitters and "caretakers." Youngsters need people who are accustomed to their "quirks" and sensitivities; preferably live-in relatives who are alert, accessible, willing and capable of ascertaining when something is "off," ready to step in, pre-emptively if necessary, and remove these youngsters from situations they cannot handle.

A "neutral bureaucrat" (that is to say, a child-care professional, or a "child protective services agent") cannot fill this role, no matter how well-meaning or dedicated. Whereas, some children (but probably not many) may play an occasional violent video game or listen to graphic rap lyrics without experiencing nightmares or other emotional ramifications, thousands more youngsters find these experiences troubling, upsetting or at least memorable, whether they ever act on disturbing content or not.

Unsettling sexual images and violent literature act as "negative triggers." This tends to interrupt the latency period, the time during which a child typically absorbs the concept of compassion (according to, among other sources, the late Melvin Anchell, M.D., who was called in numerous times to testify as an expert in court cases, including for the government). This trigger sits there, in the subconscious mind, simmering over time, and frequently contributes, in some future time-frame, to a psychological "fall" or "lapse," particularly if a second trigger-event emerges.

The now-older child may have forgotten the exact nature of the original incident. But at the point a lapse occurs, it will take all the skill of a caring adult—whether a parent, a pastor, a friend, or a psychotherapist—to ferret out that first "negative trigger," never mind trying to "fix" it. There is no pill, no medical antidote that exists to erase a "negative trigger." Some adolescents and young adults try self-medicating, using, say, painkillers, tranquilizers or alcohol. But any perceived relief is short-lived, and the anguish returns—unless the individual is able, at some point, to intellectualize it and, as the saying goes, "move on."

Wise parents of young children and adolescents prohibit and/or intercept violent video games; ugly, demeaning rap lyrics; pornography; and literature featuring repeated graphic language. They are on the lookout for potentially disturbing (age-inappropriate) TV and Internet images. As soon as the child is able to comprehend it (the "age of reason" is thought to occur after the age of seven), parents can try to explain <u>why</u> they are taking pre-emptive steps. While parents cannot, today, completely stop the avalanche of negativity engulfing their offspring, they can severely *limit* it. Throwing in the towel due to the pervasive nature of today's culture rot is not a good game plan, and not in the interests of society.

Parents also need to introduce positive experiences rather than leaving it to the school or church. This means (horrors!) full-time parenting—something the Left, for obvious reasons, finds distasteful and regularly mocks under the umbrella of feminism and the supposed need for either two incomes or merely for the career enhancement that additional workloads bring.

Today's almost universal deficiency of full-time childrearing by parents or close relatives, coupled to the trend of cohabitation and multiple, blended families compared with forty-five years ago, has resulted in rates of depression and suicides endemic to this generation of children too high to be merely coincidental. Modern-day young people, after all, have unparalleled access to every electronic gizmo and source of entertainment imaginable, "over-the-top" birthday parties, chauffeured proms to fancy places (as opposed to the proverbial high-school gym decked out in crepe paper), and computerized social networks. This is quite unlike the plight of youngsters of the 1930s, '40s, '50s, and even '60s. In those eras, schoolchildren of all ages had more limited entertainment options, a myriad of expected daily chores, world wars and economic depressions that consumed any "down-time." The presence of guns and other munitions was an established fact of life in nearly every household. Yet somehow, with rare exceptions, yesterday's children thrived, and incidents of random, mass killing sprees were almost unheard of. Isolated fights, murders and bank-robbery-type conduct by "outlaw" groups, as they used to be called, became the stuff of legends, of course, but you could just about count them on one hand.

The Ethics of Nonjudgmentalism

The current—and preferred—ethical climate of "situational ethics" for collegiates and new job applicants boils down to the following:

- There is no right or wrong, only conditioned responses.
- The collective good is more important than the individual.
- Consensus is more important than principle.
- Flexibility is more important than accomplishment.
- Nothing is permanent except change.
- All ethics are situational; there are no moral absolutes.
- There are no perpetrators, only victims.

The mantra of "nonjudgmentalism" is key to this ethical system. It has morphed into an acceptance of nearly everything, while "zero tolerance" has assumed a grotesque and hypocritical irrationality. The schoolchildren of the 1940s and '50s carried small bottles of aspirin, cold medications and even legitimate prescriptions in their purses and pockets with neither harassment nor misuse. The illicit recreational drug craze that began in the late 1960s and '70s in no way necessitated the draconian measures instituted in today's public schools. Yet, we are commanded to be "nonjudgmental," even while this ridiculous hypocrisy is carried out under our noses.

Today, *non-judgmentalism* even extends to justification of old Soviet gulags, early sexual liaisons, and riots passed off as "peaceable assemblies." "Controlled" discussions concerning such things abound in social studies and "health" classes, to the detriment of millions of youngsters who suffer the consequences—including traumatic sexual encounters, gang rapes and drug-induced crime sprees. Some high school teachers have stated that in a course covering the Holocaust, students rationalized that Nazi atrocities "made sense" given the state of the German economy at the time. This skewed view of reality has a basis; it is the rare high-school student who gets a more complete view of German history—from, say, 1700 to the present, including the population's exposure to Judeo-Christian values and morality.

So, with their non-judgmentalism now intact, students take on issues ranging from capital punishment of violent predators to "renditioning" of terrorists, and the horror of "blood diamonds"—mostly because it is popular to do so, and because they see these issues raised in the movies, works intended more to entertain than to inform.

Now you can hold any views you like on capital punishment "renditioning," and the cruel methods sometimes employed to extract diamonds from mines in Africa. But whatever conclusions you may have come to on these hopefully come with a background and context. In the case high-schoolers, encouraged by the teacher to engage in class discussion without any thorough grounding in fact-based, chronological history, there is a disparity of arguments; cause-effect are not aligned. On the one hand, the students are rationalizing Nazi atrocities and, in practically the same breath, they are rejecting capital punishment in murder cases—with no historical context for either one. This shows a stunning lack of logic.

"Deculturization" and Social Pressure

Cliques and peer pressure are nothing new. But the trend toward the kind of vicious bullying you read about today is linked to "nonjudgmentalism" and mandated political correctness in that both feature trendy, voluntary self-disclosure coupled to a disconnect between cause and effect. Nonjudgmentalism has become part and parcel of today's pop culture, with roots in, ironically, *sensitivity coaching*, which we will be taking up in the next section. Among adults, these have morphed into harassment-prevention workshops, diversity training and various "tolerance" programs in the workplace. Terms like "harassment-prevention," "diversity," and "tolerance," of course are all euphemisms, and the repeated hype surrounding the terminologies inspire more incidents, in the old vicious cycle. This may seem psychologically perverse, but such is the result of "conditioning." Professional molders of public opinion (including public relations advisors and marketing agents) know that "conditioning" is what repetitive media hype does best. Recall in Section 5 of the Beginner course: Barack Obama's early-on Chief of Staff, Rahm Emanuel, once quipping: ". . . never let a serious crisis go to waste." Recall also the principle of psych-war about "creating conditions" for purposes of exploitation in the future.

The glue that holds the ugliest side of the crisis-manufacturing business together is "deculturization"—the removal and abandonment of one's own culture and replacement with another, more alien one. The term *culture* in this context includes art, literature, music, prevalent value system (usually religiously based), political *baseline* (that is, a nation's "default," or "starting position," as in our country's Constitution, Declaration of Independence and Bill or Rights), and any predominating philosophy of life (such as "hard work and education are the tickets to success"). If you examine all these components of what used to be called "the American way of life" over the past forty-five years, you will notice that our culture has been stripped away, one piece at a time.

"De-Nazification": The Launch-Pad for *Deculturization*

The concept of *deculturization* is not new; conquering armies even prior to biblical times did it all the time—although it was never specifically referred to by that term, nor did it have a specific process associated with doing so. But with the fall of the Third Reich after World War II, the term was jump-started using an aggressive program of German "de-Nazification," set up by the Allies.

The Communists, by that time, were not exactly on our BFF ("best friends forever") list, but they incorporated and refined many of the techniques applied to the West's de-Nazification efforts. Herbert Marcuse, the German double-agent-turned American campus-protest organizer, was key among the principal contributors to America's deculturization and Constitution-detractors. How Marcuse went from being the darling of the Office of Strategic Services (OSS), the Office of War Information (OWI), and its later incarnation, the Central Intelligence Agency (CIA), hand-picked by America's political leaders to coordinate the "rehabilitation" of Nazi Germany (he never even returned to live in his native Germany after the war), to becoming one of the most accomplished traitors and double-agents in the world, makes for fascinating reading all by itself. Although largely forgotten today—and certainly not written up in college textbooks—he was, perhaps, *the* single most significant major-player in the left-wing campaign to deculturize America.

Marcuse gives us a first-hand look at the connection between the Berlin-based Frankfurt School—(a.k.a. Institute for Social Research (ISR)—and Josef Stalin's brand of communist agitation, which utilized anarchy as a strategy (inciting riots, mass demonstrations, rock-throwing protests, among other things).

The ISR was launched in 1923 by a group of Marxist intellectuals in Germany—in other words, prior to World War II—thereby providing the link between a rising Third Reich in Germany and Lenin's brand of Marxism. Marcuse wound up playing both sides during Stalin's era, and so virtually redefined what we *mis*interpret today as *right-wing* versus *left-wing*. In reality, they are two sides of the same coin. Taking his cue from both the Nazis and the communists—a little bit of this and a little bit of that—Marcuse turned our Western ideals 180 degrees toward a socialist and bureaucratic mentality.

American intelligence had thought that because the Third Reich caused Marcuse's meteoric career to be blocked early on (because of his Jewish heritage)—first, he tried currying favor through the ISR (in Berlin), then found himself on the run, first to Geneva and then to the United States, with a seeming offer of service—he would be the perfect candidate to head up de-Nazification efforts.

They couldn't have been more wrong.

Our nation was completely unprepared for the kinds of psychological warfare unleashed in Marcuse's wake. He had plenty of help, of course, from like-minded, well-known political theorists of his day, all of them individuals with a radical bent. Among them were Max Horkheimer, Theodor Adorno, Walter Benjamin, Erich Fromm, Friedrich Pollock, Leo Löwenthal and Jürgen Habermas.

Marcuse merged his theory of "repressive tolerance" (the extension of tolerance to policies, attitudes and opinions which are outlawed or suppressed by the prevailing population) with the "consensus" strategies of his contemporary, German philosopher Georg Wilhelm Frederich Hegel around 1932. So, Hegel was actually the originator of the phony consensus methods we studied in the Beginner Course. Recall, that a practiced manipulator takes one firm point of view and then its opposite, combines them, and comes up with a brand, new viewpoint—a synthesis of the two—which all parties will accept as if they had thought of it on their own.

Marcuse took the trouble to revise many early interpretations of Marxism so that they would appeal to young American college intellectuals; in fact, at least three of his writings, *Eros and Civilization*, *Reason and Revolution*, and *One-Dimensional Man*, were routinely circulated among student protesters—even pressed into their hands—at many of the demonstrations he helped organize. Many aging Boomers who were former campus radicals confirm this today.

SECTION 3

The Self-Disclosure Craze

Two key Americans from the same era (among miscellaneous others) helped to acclimate the newest K–12 set to the radicalism and ethical climate already adopted by their older siblings and classmates of the 1960s and '70s: Ralph Tyler (1902–1994) and Francis Keppel (1916–1990). Through their contributions to "assessment" under the cover of academic ("standardized") testing, and their two pet projects—the ever-expanding Elementary and Secondary Education Act of 1965 and the National Assessment of Educational Progress (NAEP)—they helped ensure that the next generation of young students would come to view intimate and personal classroom questions, interspersed among their classwork and school "tests," as standard fare.

The idea for a national assessment gained impetus in 1963, and NAEP planning began in 1964, with a grant from the Carnegie Corporation to set up the Exploratory Committee for the Assessment of Progress in Education (ECAPE) in June of that year. Ralph Tyler served as head not only of the Carnegie Foundation for part of that period, but its for-profit spinoff, the Educational Testing Service. Conveniently, Tyler also was Commissioner of Education when it was still under the auspices of the US Department of Health, Education and Welfare—shortly before the Education Department became a Cabinet-level agency in its own right. He also created many state assessments under separate contracts, modeling them on the NAEP. This was a huge conflict of interest, and both Tyler and Keppel should have been given the boot by Congress; instead, the two men were revered, showered with grant money and given free reign to reshape American education so that the state, not the parent, was in charge.

The media served as a helpmate—seemingly by coincidence, yet just at the right time to give a boost to the trend of self-disclosure. Here is how:

Beginning in the early 1980s, tabloid, "shock-rock"-style television talk shows like *The Jerry Springer Show* and *The Ricki Lake Show* made their debuts. By the 1990s, a wave of "freak shows" had become the rage. This was not Arthur Godfrey or Ed Sullivan seeking new talent and politely offering a sample of the best their talent scouts could find. Instead, the new wave of guests got fifteen minutes or so of fame by discussing their most intimate moments, including deviant and illegal behaviors.

Pro-family, traditionalist groups like the Parents Television Council and American Family Association attempted to put a stop to such lurid programming, especially inasmuch as they were clearly (and later admittedly) aimed at young viewers. It eventually became clear that additional segments of these "lowbrow" exhibitions were deliberately being aired on school holidays. The traditionalist groups appealed to sponsors to pull their advertising. But they were way too late at that point, and had virtually no clout with advertisers, who were looking only at their "bottom line." *The Oprah Winfrey Show*, already popular, expanded its tabloid-type interviews to include whatever was salaciously intimate in 1993.

All this had a secondary effect on the education establishment, whose luminaries had been leaning ever more leftward, and becoming increasingly jealous of parental prerogatives since the 1970s. Suddenly, "assessment type" questioning of students, featuring intimate and personal details was acceptable, and requirements for signed, parental consent were virtually ignored. When parents complained, they got the run-around, whereas in the 1950s, such an outrage would have never been tolerated. (See Appendix. Also note that many examples of personal questions, complete with computer links to proof concerning the federal agencies responsible, have appeared in previous works by this author.)

To exemplify the growing acceptance of self-disclosure between the 1950s and the '80s, we can flash back in time to the 1970s and a television "contest" called *The Gong Show*. It was rejected by the public because it was deemed insulting to contestants! One has to ask how such a turnabout evolved; why embarrassing self-disclosures became suddenly acceptable, and even "courageous." Teen magazines routinely carry intimate, personal surveys, which youngsters are supposed to snail-mail (or email) in, supposedly anonymously, for tabulation of the more scandalous responses to questions.

Today, *The Gong Show* would be respectable (recall Herbert Marcuse's "theory of repressive tolerance" a few pages back). Today, the old *Gong Show* has morphed into *American Idol*, *The Voice*, and other productions which insult guests and mimic—even promote—the kinds of malicious bullying we read and hear about in schools (under so-called "no tolerance" policies!), and they condition young people into a "tell-all" and "reporting on family, friends and neighbors" mentality—the more embarrassing, the better. This makes it ever easier for school staff and other extensions of government, as well as human-resources agents at major companies, to engage in politicized spying via questionnaires, surveys and "tests." Mental-health surveys and questionnaires in public schools health classes are ubiquitous—with intimate questions about sex (and sexual attraction), drugs (whose, when and why), religious beliefs (*not* merely naming the denomination or sect, but specific tenets and practices of the faith), parental teachings (their magazine subscriptions and what they do for fun), depression, etc.

If, as a parent, you discover and push the issue, you will be told that the state has a ***compelling interest*** in collecting such information. The "compelling interest" justification also allows the introduction of controversial and even offensive lesson units, say on homosexuality, to be introduced into elementary school classrooms as young as first grade. Whereas, federal regulations once precluded government interference in choices of curriculum in local schools (Public law 92-318, Sec.432 and P.L. 96-88, Title I, Sec. 101, no. 3), they got around these with "compelling state interest."

For example, halting the spread of sexually transmitted diseases (STDs) is a compelling state interest, but teaching basic reading, science or math, are not. As to what are called "the basics," the government eventually put out a "Best Practices" document through the US Department of Education, which came with political pressure—the kind that meant the "best" ways were the "politically correct" ways to avoid federal and state funding being withheld.

So, all this, together, laid the groundwork for today's current fixation on "self-disclosure." Tell-all chatter works particularly well with kids because they like to talk about themselves. As for the rest of us, we are conditioned to crave the kinds of adulation that media "stardom" (including scandal) brings, if only for fifteen minutes.

This is a "win-win" situation for political entities with an ulterior agenda.

Moreover, people today casually expose their subconscious thoughts, and in so doing they respond to the psychological stimulus of pseudo-importance. Social media has taken this capability, literally, to the outer limits.

In an era of oversensitivity—can Awareness of Acne Week be far behind?—this, too, is stunning. It's a set-up, again, for a psychological fall: A populace that routinely engages in self-disclosure behaviors, as well as those who eagerly devour them, will come to accept massive domestic spying by government. In fact, we have already done so.

Because today's political correctness—via projects like the Resident Assistant programs in various universities (Advanced Course, Section 3)—dictates that "authorities" and "officials" should actually be notified concerning "inappropriate" viewpoints and opinions, the First Amendment is virtually ripped from the Constitution, as university administrators, employers, corporative executives and even agents of government (bureaucrats) become less sensitive about cutting short a budding career on the basis of nebulous causes, even cross-matching any information collected for ulterior purposes.

SECTION 4

Sensitivity and Encounter Group (Training)

"Sensitivity" and "encounter" programming are designed to obliterate the individualistic streak carried around by most of us to a greater or lesser degree, and to replace it with a need for approval from the group. As per an earlier discussion, a successfully "de-sensitized" individual will need his peers more his principles. Another goal of de-sensitization is to acclimate large masses of individuals to relish something that, left to their own devices, most would not want at all.

How "Sensitivity Training" Works

Sensitivity training, encounter groups (a.k.a. T-groups) work from the same basis: They induce artificial stress, pressure and anxiety among participants who suddenly (and usually unexpectedly) find themselves defending themselves against vicious accusations.

Trainers select any one of several hot-button topics over a period of days or weeks, and one by one, target individuals in the group who appear be vulnerable, either on the subject in question, or because of their personality. This person will be singled out and interrogated, in the manner of "bullying." Once the "subject" becomes visibly upset, the rest of the group is incited to scream accusations and hurl insults at the targeted individual.

The National Training Laboratory, a venture of the teachers' union behemoth, the aforementioned National Education Association (NEA), is the major training ground for professional agitation, provocation, and inducing social change. The NTL introduced terms like "**change-agent skills**" and "**freezing/unfreezing of attitudes**." These terms are used liberally today. Among the first training texts was *Training for Change Agents*, aimed at teachers, by Ronald G. and Mary C. Havelock in 1976. One of the more eye-popping subheadings is *"**Extinguishing Existing Attitudes, Knowledge, and Behaviors in the Person**"* (p. 44). One has to ask: Why would a teacher need to know that?

The original text carried an Institute for Social Research (ISR) background watermark on the cover, which means, you may recall, the Frankfurt School, as per an earlier discussion in this section on double-agent and communist campus organizer, Herbert Marcuse. (The ISR now has branches in universities across the United States.) In any case, *Training for Change Agents* is easily accessible in the giant Educational Resource Information Center (ERIC) database, which indicates the text is now legitimized. You may still be able to obtain a used copy at an on-line bookstore. For years, however, it was tightly held and rarely acknowledged.

In *Issues in (Human Relations) Training*, NEA editors wrote in 1952 that sensitivity training "fits into a context of . . . coercive persuasion. . . ." David Jenkins' essay in the same issue of the publication explained that the laboratories conducted by NTL had moved from "skill training" to "sensitivity training," and that "the trainer has no alternative but to manipulate"; and to "produce behavior" that "create[s] changes in other people." Needless to say, such admissions would not have sat well with the public in 1952, which is why they were kept under wraps.

Origins of "T-Groups"

Under whichever name they go—"T-Groups, Sensitivity Training or Encounter Sessions—the methods are based in Nazi-era German psychologist Kurt Lewin's "group dynamics" and on Soviet neuropsychologist Alexander Luria's major research paper, "Artificial Disorganization of Behavior." Both Luria's and Lewin's methods were originally tested on prisoners of war, on home-grown soldiers in their two countries and on prison convicts.

Kurt Lewin emigrated from Germany to the United States in the 1930s, and it was his students who helped establish the NTL. But Kurt Lewin was a mover and shaker in Great Britain before he ever got to America—and was no ordinary refugee from Germany, either. Lewin was among the first of many infiltrators who accumulated grant money from various foundations and from the US government to pursue psychological manipulation experiments that would eventually target our own citizens and those of the free world.

Luria and Lewin came to the same conclusions regarding coerced consensus-building: that individuals representing varied backgrounds and personalities could be manipulated by a "group leader" (a.k.a facilitator) into launching a formerly unacceptable "consensus" of opinion, *provided* they could trick these individuals into taking on a new "group identity." This requires the application of controlled stress and social pressure. Humiliation of the "subject" is an especially helpful form of social pressure; often the targeted person (or persons) will later deny that any change has taken place. The victim may even walk away without knowing that his position on an issue has changed.

The key to the process is, again, the creation of a controlled environment, with imposition of stress being the key. But what this means for America is that the NEA-based NTL programs (remember, this is basically a *teachers' union*, passing itself off as a "professional association" aimed at improving the nation's schools) has been operating under both Nazi and old Soviet Communist banners. When you research quotes from NEA leaders of the late 1940s through the 1970s (e.g., former NEA executive secretary Willard Givens, and past NEA presidents Elizabeth Koontz, George Fischer, and Catharine Barrett), you will find that they were not particularly subtle or secretive about their views.

Under the rubric of "sociometry" and "sociodrama," passed off under the more benign term "role-playing," they brought sensitivity training into classrooms filled with vulnerable children. This particular form of role-playing wasn't at all the innocent exercise usually associated with that term. Psychiatrist Jacob L. Moreno (1889–1974) made the initial forays into school curriculum with his "group psychotherapy-as-sociodrama," coining the term "sociometry" to describe it. Today, Moreno has found new respectability as the foremost "pioneer" of group psychotherapy and "transactional analysis."

What it was, in professional circles, was the infamous "forced-choice technique." In Moreno's 1953 tome, *Who Shall Survive?*, subtitled *Foundations of Sociometry, Group Psychotherapy and Sociodrama*, he incorporated sensitivity training methodology and praised John Dewey for introducing psychological techniques into elementary and secondary education.

Moreno's methods were developed into more hard-hitting fare for children by Hilda Taba in the early 1960s with considerable federal funding from the federal government via San Francisco State College.

Humanistic education advocate, Jane Howard, penned the book *Please Touch: A Guide Tour of the Human Potential Movement* (McGraw-Hill, NY, 1970). This not only provided a closer look at "humanistic psychology"—not to be confused with *humane,* as per Section 10 of the Intermediate Course—but carried what became a standard rationale for "T-groups": ". . . human potential groups [are] striving to reacquaint us with the 'affective domain,' and help us to be less 'cognitive.'"

We already discussed how the term *cognitive* came to be redefined, also in Section 10 of the Intermediate Course. "Affective," in educator circles, means the emotive, or feeling, part our mind, which, as we have already learned, came to be favored over the intellect. For pupils, this meant they would become more reactive (as in "knee-jerk" responses) than analytical or logical. Small groups, in Jane Howard's view, were key to the leftist version of "humanist" success. This dovetails with the axiom set out at the beginning of this course: *It's easier to control a group than to control an individual.*

By the end of 1970, psychologically coercive methods like sensitivity training were in full swing throughout most public schools, even before the cabinet-level agency emerged in 1976, which, you may recall, happens to be the same year the Havelocks' *Training for Change Agents* text was published.

A critique of sensitivity training by Clifford Edwards explains how "disillusionment and value disintegration" and establishment of "group values" (this is where "unfreezing" and "freezing" of attitudes comes in) causes youngsters to dissociate from parents and other adults. Encounter "games" like Magic Circle emerged—contrived exercises aimed at self-disclosure and attitudinal change via politicized curricula that parents never saw in their children's textbooks: nuclear war scenarios in which students choose which loved one to leave out of a bomb shelter, parents portrayed as greedy materialists, and "guided imagery" (based on hypnosis) into sexual fantasies. In other words, these were lessons, often on mimeographed paper, that had nothing to do with academic truth, reading, writing, arithmetic, science or literature.

All this had the effect of encouraging youngsters to focus on each other instead of looking to leadership and guidance from their parents and other established role-models of the era, such as pastors and police. Remember these were children, sitting as a "captive audience," not adults willingly going to see a psychotherapist and paying for services. We see the results today in the form of "sexting," casual "hook-ups," and vicious bullying, as well as in an appalling loss of decorum, propriety, tact and civility.

Grit Your Teeth and Bear It

How has all this played out? Let's take, for example, "rap music": To pull off an appreciation of this genre nationwide—regardless of any racial or ethnic considerations—requires more than one or two cute songs (such as "Who Let the Dogs Out," which always draws a smile). Ignore that much of the genre is demeaning to women and uses crass (not to mention insensitive) language: It is loud and intellectually disjointed. You can't hum or whistle a rendition of it as you go about your chores. Rap has no musicality or harmony, only a beat and is typically an emotional downer.

Another example, is nonstop TV dramas depicting graphic carnage and blood, whether the plot is interesting or not. Intentionally or not, most people view hour-after-hour of gore and guts.

A third example is universal pat-downs; invasive baggage checks without probable cause are routine on all air travelers, 100 percent of the time.

All three examples above would not have been tolerated in a pre-1970s America. This is so far removed from the "love-and-peace" generation of 1960s-era Baby Boomers that even many of the most "hip" of the hippie movement say their reaction to these things is an urge to throw up.

Countless people initially walked out of shopping malls and health clubs that played rap "music." At first, some used Walkman-type devices and earphones to block out the noise, then moved to iPods and "earbuds" as they became available. Still, the overly loud "stimuli" of rap came through and made most folks irritable and nervous, and most weren't shy about saying so. But eventually, Americans became "de-sensitized" and just put up with it.

Similarly, people left theaters, changed channels or just did something else after an hour or two of bloody television dramas. They wrote to sponsors. Parents previewed shows that their children might watch. The V-chip was invented to help parents screen out inappropriate TV material. But by the time the gore had reached even into daytime cartoons, they gave up, shifted their gaze during disturbing graphic scenes or tried to ignore it—and finally, by the early 2000s, became "de-sensitized."

Similarly, after thousands of complaints about the TSA, which were summarily ignored or rebuffed, and despite well-circulated camera-phone snapshots and YouTube videos circulating the Internet, without a single serious investigation of any specific complaint, the uproar died down. Even former Minnesota Governor Jesse Ventura attempted a lawsuit. It went nowhere.

Various expensive programs aimed at allowing upstanding citizens to bypass TSA lines went broke (such as Clear®), and people finally just gritted their teeth and put up with it. Today, they are acclimated to bureaucratic excess. The travel rate by plane has never been higher.

De-sensitization of the type described in the examples above functions *as a gauge of public resistance*. A test. Much of the apparent apathy is mainly a result of repetition and sloganizing, with a bit of intimidation thrown in. It is easy to recognize all three as ingredients of encounter-style conditioning, which of course is the basis of sensitivity training.

Scary Journey

Some people either freely enroll in sensitivity programs and training courses, or they are "tapped" for training, as in, *being invited*. The sales-pitch to potential enrollees is that they have hidden potential, and that they will embark on "a journey of self-discovery," "diversity facilitation," and "quality-management training." Training grounds are entities such as the International Institute for Applied Behavioral Sciences; NEA's National Training Lab (now known as the NTL Institute for Applied Behavioral Sciences, based in Rosslyn, Virginia, and its West Coast base of operations, the Western Training Laboratories in Group Development), and Esalen Institute (also originally set up by the NTL, but now independent).

It is estimated that in the past forty years, several million have gone through one of these T-group doors. Participants have included many of the nation's corporate leaders. Similar programs have even been run for the State Department, the US Navy, the US Department of Education, and other agencies of the federal bureaucracy.

So, if you ever wonder how the goliath teacher's union, the NEA, managed to amass so much power, to exert so much influence over two generations, and to virtually change American society, look no further than the sensitivity programs inaugurated by these master manipulators.

SECTION 5

Tale of Two Tavistocks

The Tavistock Method and the National Training Lab converge in that they both make use of Kurt Lewin's "Group Dynamics"-*cum*-sensitivity training, Alexander Luria's "Artificial Disorganization"-*cum*-thought disruption, and encounter-style techniques of controlled stress as a form of group "therapy" to change social and political attitudes and achieve "consensus."

The Tavistock Method, however, is considerably more harsh in that it got its start under the cover of actual medicine, then assumed the banner of "Human Relations" to gain credibility and legitimacy among Western, especially American, institutions. Its methods were funded in Britain and America by many of the usual suspects on the Left listed in the Introduction to the Advanced Course under "Institutes, Associations, Foundations and NGOs."

There is an understandable confusion as to the differences and similarities between the *Tavistock Institute of Human Relations, Tavistock Clinic* and the *Tavistock Centre for Couple Relationships (TCCR)*. Much of the information to clear up this muddle comes from the superb research of Dr. Dennis L. Cuddy, who has chronicled the Tavistock entities, its major players, and how each converted high-stress brainwashing techniques into covert manipulation strategies with broad applications. All eventually learned to "hang their hat" on the hook of psychotherapeutic services (i.e., family relationships, prevention of family breakdown, couples counseling, adolescent counseling, etc.) in order to garner grants from government agencies and charitable donors. Today, for example, TCCR aligns with the United Kingdom Council for Psychotherapy and the British Association for Counselling and Psychotherapy, and is headquartered in London.

The Tavistock industries can be looked upon as outgrowths of the *Tavistock Institute of Medical Psychology*, founded in 1920. Back then, Tavistock Institute and the Clinic were pretty much one and the same. But in 1945, the Clinic drew the attention of Rockefeller Medical Director Alan Gregg, who toured various institutions that had been involved in wartime medicine to see if any group would be willing to commit to an extension of enemy-analysis research in social psychiatry *and apply it to civilian populations.* Tavistock Clinic was.

According to the *official* history (meaning the PR) of the Tavistock Clinic:

Its 1920 founding was launched under Dr. Crichton-Miller's leadership. The Clinic made a significant contribution to the understanding of the traumatic effects of "shell shock" and how it could be treated by talking, listening and understanding. The Clinic, through charitable funding, also supposedly provided mental health treatment to the general population, based primarily on Freudian psychological approaches.

A subsequent grant was awarded by the Rockefeller Foundation and resulted in a redirected Tavistock, the Tavistock Institute of Human Relations, founded in 1946. One year following the end of World War II, it separated (at least on paper) from the Tavistock Clinic and concerned itself almost exclusively with group and organizational behavior. Jock Sutherland became director of the "new," post-war Tavistock Clinic, and it was incorporated into a freshly established British National Health Service that same year.

But key figures from the Clinic were still allied and actively involved with Tavistock Institute, and they brought their research with them: Kurt Lewin, who proceeded to head up the Frankfurt School/ISR in America, brought along his work in "group dynamics." John D. Sutherland, John Bowlby, Eric Trist, and Fred Emery incorporated their work. John Rawlings Rees, who was instrumental in obtaining the Rockefeller grant to create the Institute in the first place, became first president of the World Federation for Mental Health. Former Clinic bigwig, Ronald Hargreaves, went on to become deputy director of the World Health Organization, and Tommy Wilson became chairman of the Tavistock Institute.

The "new" Tavistock began publishing the international journal, *Human Relations,* which, contrary to the title's implication, provides an eye-popping historical record of "improvements" to what was admittedly called *thought control* and *thought reform* (a.k.a. *re-education*). According to its website, the Institute engages in educational research, and consultancy work in the social sciences and applied psychology. Its clients are chiefly *public sector organizations*, which is mightily important to us as a free-world country, and includes even the European Union, several British government agencies, and a few private (influential) clients. With credibility like that allowed to establish itself, the chances of traditionalists, privacy advocates or constitutionalists (even libertarians) mounting the kind of resistance it would take today to weaken Tavistock's hold is slim-to-none. It would take everything we have, and then some.

Other names closely associated with the Institute can be found in university-level history books, online (to an extent) and in libraries: Melanie Klein, Carl Gustav Jung, J. A. Hadfield, Charles Rycroft, Wilfred Bion, and R. D. Laing. None believed in personal independence in the spirit of the American founders, or even liked British reformists leaning toward individual rights and privacy. These men and women literally turned Britain into the socialist welfare state it is today, with forays into "security" that are just now making their appearance in US hidden surveillance cameras. They were influential in generating thousands of new regulations that work against average citizens, and waged a virtual war against personal self-defense. All are now part of the British system.

Those interested in a deeper understanding of various other shades of radicalism brought to bear on the issues of thought control and re-education, so successfully carried out and inflicted on the Britain people, would be advised to look into each of the individuals named above.

John Rawlings Rees and Experiments in Mass Neurosis

John Rawlings Rees (1890–1969), who finally assumed the title of British Brigadier General, has the distinction of being one of the most malevolent characters in history. How bad? Historical records confirm that, along with Henry Dicks, another kingpin of the Tavistock Clinic group, Rees was charged with the care of Hitler's Deputy Rudolf Hess at the secret prison locations where he was held following his escape and subsequent capture in Scotland. Between June 1941 up to Hess's appearance at the Nuremberg trial, Rees apparently established a relationship with Hess. Hess's diaries record many meetings with Rees, referred to at this time as Colonel Rees, in which Hess accused his captors of attempting to poison, drug, and 'mesmerize' him.

Rees was a colleague and admirer of Kurt Lewin, except that he went even further, developing the vicious Tavistock Method of "creating a psychological environment." Rees found that if he applied a combination of agitation and stress in just the right proportions, he could usually force (not simply encourage) pervasive changes of attitude in many people at once, by provoking hysteria and inducing what he called mass "neurosis." He once boasted that he could take a roomful of rational adults and turn them into the equivalent of whimpering children.

Unsurprisingly, Rees gained consultative status even with the United Nations, which effectively turned that body into a rubber-stamp entity for worldwide socialism, Marxist-Leninism, and now provides a safe haven for terrorism to thrive. The UN elevates the worst abusers on the planet to head its Human Rights Council, in the misguided "hope"—if you put the best face on it—that something resembling a human rights mentality will "rub off" on the miscreant.

Tavistock Clinic Aligns with the British National Health Service (NHS)

Tavistock Clinic was named for its original location in Tavistock Square, Bloomsbury, and became a noted "centre for psychoanalytic therapy" in the British National Health Service (NHS). The public relations goes that the clinic offered outpatient services in London and provided postgraduate training and academic courses for professionals in mental health, social care and organizational consulting.

Many of the Clinic's professional staff had joined the armed services as psychiatric specialists, where some (notably Dr. Wilfred Bion) introduced radical new methods of selecting officers, using the "leaderless group" as an instrument to observe which men should be given responsibility. This led to reductions in the number of applicants rejected—and to politically correct extremism.

His methods made their way to America.

So, if you wonder why a decorated Army officer like Lt. Colonel Matthew Dooley, who was tasked in 2013 with instructing leaders at the Joint Forces Staff College on the thinking underlying methods used by this nation's current enemies—a multitude of "jihadist" Middle Eastern terrorist organizations—was castigated by General Martin E. Dempsey simply for providing the pro-forma overview of a "know-thy-enemy" crash course, look no further than Tavistock, which now marches in lock-step with the UN's views on political correctness. The mere allusion to "radical Islam" or "militant Middle Eastern terrorist organizations" is *verboten*, whereas any suggestion of Christian favoritism (as in attempting to keep a long-standing exhibit of the Ten Commandments along the entranceway to a courthouse) is fair game.

Moreover, wartime experiences still influence the Tavistock Clinic's worldwide teachings, and Tavistock influence continues to underscore political correctness in US policymaking. Its advocacy of early childhood separation from parents, for example, was taken from the necessary evacuation of children during World War II, just as its treatment of trauma now extends to "sensitivity" workshops based on Tavistock bigwig Kurt Lewin's work.

The Tavistock trio, in all its incarnations, can be considered as a pioneer in promoting behavioral science along Freudian lines and "controlling" humans beings. It has established its ideology worldwide. Its network extends from the University of Sussex to the United States through the Stanford Research Institute, Esalen, and corporations such as Rand and Mitre, among others. (In America, for example, the Rand Corporation was commissioned by the old US Office of Education under the US Department of Health, Education and Welfare to pen a five-volume 1975 series of change agent texts on education entitled *Federal Programs Supporting Educational Change*. Volume II, in particular, left no room for misinterpretation of intention, with its revealing title: *Factors Affecting Change Agent Projects*.)

One can't help but be disturbed by the ironic reality that the Tavistock entities distinguished themselves by studying the effect of shell shock on British soldiers and establishing the "breaking point" of men under stress—mostly under the direction of the British Army Bureau of Psychological Warfare, commanded by Sir/Brigadier General John Rawlings Rees.

Behind the Scenes Summary

In summation, our present predicament in countering group manipulation has its roots in amoral foreign radicals, individuals and organizations that future generations may be able to look up if they can still find the names, but which will never appear in a required college text of history and may well become lost to those who want to re-light the fires of our American Founders' vision for our country under constitutional law. The culprits, which most American high school and college graduates never even heard of, include Wilhelm Wundt, Otto Gross, Wilhelm Steckel, Max Horkheimer, Erich Fromm, Wilhelm Reich, Kurt Lewin, Friedrich Engels, Karl Marx, Herbert Marcuse, Walter Benjamin, and Theodor Adorno (all of German origin); Robert Owen, A.S. Neill, Havelock Ellis, John Rawlings Rees, and A. J. Orage (of British origin); Sigmund Freud in Austria; Dr. Brock Chisholm in Canada; Antonio Gramsci of Italy; and Anatoly Lunacharsky and Georg Lukacs of Russia. These were the key figures who triggered the deculturization of the United States. Of these men, most people recognize only the names of Engels, Marx and Freud. But it was primarily the work and theories of the other individuals in the foregoing list that were the source of today's obsession with casual, noncommital sex; the rejection of the paternal family; the denigration of authority; the eradication of religion; and the stigmatization of the character ethic. The quotation below needs no elaboration:

> We were trained in all phases of warfare, both psychological and physical, for the destruction of the Capitalistic society and Christian civilization. In one portion of our studies we went thoroughly into the matter of psychopolitics. This was the art of capturing the minds of a nation through brainwashing and fake mental health. . . . During the past few years I have noted with horror the increase of psychopolitical warfare upon the American public.
> —Kenneth Goff, member of the US Communist Party, 1936 to 1939

SELF-TEST SECTION

Self-Tests

MULTIPLE CHOICE: Select the <u>best</u> answer(s) for each question. (Unless otherwise indicated, there may be more than one, "none of the above," or "all of the above.") Answer keys are at the end.

1. **Why do parents with traditional values tend to lose when they try to reason with professional facilitators in their school districts?**

   a. Because they are thinking "me," not "we."

   b. Because most have never studied the principles of rhetoric (logic).

   c. Because they don't know that teachers and administrators have been "prepped" ahead of time to expect "nutty" parents to assail them and/or school policies.

   d. Because they mistakenly believe that teachers and other members of the Education Establishment are truly interested in being their partners.

   e. Because most lay citizens don't think like marketing agents.

   f. All of the above.

2. **What is the <u>primary</u> reason (select one) why "concerned citizen" groups get confused when they serve on task forces, committees and focus groups?**

   a. Because lay citizens tend to be shy about speaking their mind.

   b. Because average citizens tend to be overly impressed by a facilitator's credentials.

   c. Because parents and lay citizens rarely insist on being heard.

   d. Because laypersons typically don't understand consensus-building strategies.

   e. Because moderators of the discussion won't listen to participants' legitimate concerns.

3. **The <u>two</u> most important keys to controlling any controversial discussion are:**

   a. To bide your time; wait for an opportune moment to inject comments.
   b. To deprive the opposition of any chance to control the debate, or agenda.
   c. To know who is funding the opposition.
   d. To ensure that lots of people from your side participate in the discussion.
   e. To arrive armed with plenty of documentation that proves your position.
   f. To be continually deceptive and evasive in your comments.

4. **What is meant by an ancient Chinese text on battle strategy regarding the need "to drive the enemy's leaders mad"?**

   a. Blatant hypocrisy can work in your favor.
   b. You can frustrate people enough that some will sound hysterical and be discredited by the rest of the group.
   c. It is possible to create an environment where nothing makes sense.
   d. You can cause your enemy to squander his resources by contradicting himself.
   e. All of the above.

5. **The <u>long-term</u> reason (select <u>one</u>) for generating a phony consensus on an issue is:**

   a. To prove to higher-ups that this consensus is what the lay community, or group, really wants.
   b. To get group members mad at each other so they can't solve anything.
   c. To create an "irreconcilable conflict."
   d. To confuse the issue.
   e. To promote their own viewpoint.

6. **A resentful, "knee-jerk" reaction among committee participants is helpful to leftist radicals <u>primarily</u> because (choose one):**

   a. It creates chaos.
   b. It causes "thought disruption."

c. It permits the government to impose more regulations and increase red tape.

d. It allows crimes to be federalized.

e. It pits political activists against each other.

7. **In tailoring radical causes for the media (print or electronic), the <u>most</u> important consideration *to left-leaning opponents* is (select one):**

a. Getting out the facts—at least their version of the facts.

b. The psychological impact of the promotional materials.

c. Maintaining credibility.

d. Regrouping and recouping any losses.

8. **Particularly in matters of education, what <u>two</u> factors have put conservatives, traditionalists and constitutionalists at the <u>greatest</u> disadvantage?**

a. We care how many people get hurt and our opposition doesn't.

b. The opposition has secured more media outlets.

c. Our opposition can afford to go on the offensive and we can't.

d. Our adversaries view morality as a social problem instead of as a sin or a crime.

e. The police can no longer protect us.

9. **The <u>short-term</u> purposes (select two) of psychological manipulation are:**

a. To legitimize, then institutionalize, unpopular and bogus policies quickly.

b. To change the meanings of words most people thought were understood.

c. To humiliate conservatives.

d. To promote bitter confrontation between opposing factions.

10. **When a radical initiative gets a "black eye" (a bad reputation), liberal-left policymakers may do any of the following, <u>except one</u>:**

a. Change the name of the program.

b. Restructure or repackage the program and try again later.

c. Mandate the program.

d. Dump the program.

e. Replace the program with another one that is similar.

11. **Effective marketing depends upon all of the following, <u>except one</u>:**

    a. Catchy slogans.
    b. Captivating images.
    c. Factual accuracy.
    d. Appeals to accomplishment, intelligence, or fear.
    e. Targeting a specific demographic or socioeconomic market.

12. **The hardest-hitting psychological manipulation techniques were devised, or initiated, by all <u>except one</u> of the following:**

    a. Kurt Lewin
    b. The National Training Lab
    c. John Rawlings Rees
    d. The Institute for Social Research
    e. Teachers

13. **Basic axioms leftist adversaries use to create a psychological environment are:**

    a. Redefining
    b. Setting up irreconcilable conflicts
    c. Isolating the opposition
    d. Labeling opponents
    e. Repetition of key phrases and slogans
    f. All of the above

14. **In a group setting (meeting, committee, task force, etc.), you, as a knowledgeable activist, must do which <u>two</u> of the following in order to have a real voice in the discussion (i.e., to avoid being marginalized)?**

    a. Frame the debate.
    b. Have a visible network of friends with you.
    c. Bolster weaker group members to take your side.
    d. Bring a lot of information about the proposal or program with you.
    e. Distribute methods of taking on a facilitator at the meeting.

15. **A teacher promoting a particular worldview in the classroom may tell parents s/he is doing any or all of the following, <u>except</u>:**

    a. Indoctrinating pupils.
    b. Engaging in academic freedom.

c. Pursuing the right to free expression.

d. Transmitting important societal values.

16. *Surreptitious* **brainwashing and indoctrination is possible only if a facilitator has successfully accomplished which <u>two</u> tasks:**

a. Framed the debate.

b. Disrupted the victim's thought processes.

c. Rooted out a victim's emotional support system.

d. Terrorized the subject.

e. Discredited the victim.

17. **In the vernacular of professional manipulators, a *vacuum* is:**

a. A lack of any preconceived opinion on a topic.

b. A disrupted thought.

c. A stripped-out belief system.

d. Feelings of alienation and isolation.

18. **To heighten a person's suggestibility, it is necessary to:**

a. Provide a steady diet of conflicting and confusing images and words.

b. Disrupt the subject's thought process.

c. Weaken the subject's emotional support system (parents, priest, rabbi, etc.).

d. All of the above.

19. **A teacher is described by the "behaviorist" faction of educators as all the following, <u>except one</u>:**

a. A clinician

b. A facilitator of learning

c. An instructor

d. A mentor

e. A learning practitioner

20. *Educational* **indoctrination works <u>primarily</u> because:**

a. Students don't have to memorize the materials.

b. Students won't pass their courses unless they pass a test indicating they accept the new ideas.

c. Parents aren't paying attention to the lessons kids get.

d. Biased curricula bypass the conscious mind and shoot directly for the emotions.

e. The federal government is unlawfully involved in curriculum decisions.

21. **The "escape route" and "road to safety" referred to in the Principles of Psych War are best described as:**

a. Bait

b. A captive setting

c. A reprieve

d. A solution

22. **According to behaviorist-progressive educators, the <u>primary</u> role of a teacher is to:**

a. Tell children what to think

b. Teach character (values)

c. Serve as an adjunct to parents

d. Covertly influence opinions

e. Transmit knowledge

23. **One Psych War principle is "bringing one's opponent to the field of battle." To accomplish this, an adversary might:**

a. Do a negative review of a book written by the opposition in a popular publication so that people would ignore it.

b. Boldly confront us whenever we hold meetings.

c. Write letters to the editor in the city's most widely read newspaper blasting our views and candidates for office.

d. Invite a few key conservative leaders to a public meeting.

e. Turn conservatives away when they try to attend public meetings.

24. **According to the Principles of Psych War, what does it mean to "entice the enemy with something s/he is sure to take"? (Select <u>two</u>.)**

a. To lull the adversary into a false sense of security.

b. Bait, then switch tactics.

c. Ignore your opponent so that he doesn't get a forum from which to speak.

d. Have representatives of your side in as many places as possible.

e. Pretend to compromise on an issue.

25. The Republican Party is currently in disarray, with factions arguing about key issues. Turf battles have surfaced among conservative organizations, all competing for funding and/or legitimacy in the media. Which Rule of Psych War does this situation _most_ represent? (Select one.)

a. The rank-and-file are angry and have lost confidence in their leaders.

b. The numbers of registered Republicans carries little advantage.

c. The opposition has wearied its opponents by keeping them constantly occupied.

d. Accomplishment has been demanded of people who have no talent.

e. An escape route has been provided and everyone has fled.

26. What is the _most likely_ reason a facilitator inserts an irrelevant, but hot-button, comment into an argument? (Select one.)

a. To draw out and label opponents.

b. To bring attention to a point the group may have missed.

c. To divert attention from the real subject of the argument.

d. To generate more discussion among group members.

e. To subtly insert the facilitator's own opinion into the discussion.

27. Why is the following sentence considered a good marketing ploy: "This program creates a level playing field"?

a. Because it appeals to expertise.

b. Because it appeals to popularity.

c. Because it functions as a distraction.

d. Because it creates a false analogy.

e. Because it suggests "fair" and equal results.

28. If someone calls you a "fundamentalist Christian" in the course of a group discussion, you should do what? (Select _two_.)

a. Strongly deny it even if it's true.

b. Avoid denials even if it's not true.

c. Explain to everyone where the term "fundamentalist" comes from.

d. Treat it as a distraction and remind the group of the topic.

e. Discredit the person who made the allegation.

29. **The <u>three</u> keys to countering a psychological environment once it has already been established by a facilitator are:**

a. Take the "floor" and redirect the discussion.

b. Determine the real issue.

c. Locate the people who agree with you and launch a verbal counterattack.

d. Don't give the facilitator anything to work with until you have a good idea why you are really there.

e. Remember your opinion and don't get sidetracked.

30. **A facilitator/agitator's "trump card" or "operating rationale" is that:**

a. Most people never agree on anything anyway.

b. Most people are irrational and have no firm opinions.

c. Most people have never heard of a "facilitator."

d. Most people tend to agree with the moderator of a discussion.

e. Most people like to think they are rational and can work things out.

31. **Which of the following would be LEAST likely to try to hire the services of a professional facilitator to go to a community and generate a consensus for a program, project or policy?**

a. The Republican or Democratic Party headquarters

b. A nongovernmental organization (NGO)

c. A trust or endowment

d. A foundation or think-tank

e. The National Education Association

32. **Our opposition's attack strategies include all of the following, except one:**

a. The snoop survey

b. Sowing seeds (planting ideas) that de-legitimize our concerns

c. Rebutting our research point by point

d. Preparing and distributing how-to/beware manuals

e. Having the teachers' union screen all school board candidates

33. **The purpose of making sure a complainant goes through a series of proper channels in order to "process" his or her complaint is to:**

a. Get all the concerns "on the record" and "out in the open."

b. Ostracize the complainant.

c. Avoid misunderstandings and mistakes.

d. Wear down the complainant with delays and red tape.

e. Force the complainant to retract his objection.

34. **If a program, activity or policy comes under attack <u>after</u> it is implemented, the opposition's strategy may include any one of the following except the following <u>two</u>:**

a. Going on the defensive and take on the detractors.

b. Going on the offensive and vigorously promoting the program.

c. Doing away with the program.

d. Making the program "voluntary."

e. Reviewing policies for loopholes in order to retain the program.

35. **School board candidates can expect any number of questions to come up in their campaign. All of the following are possibilities, except which <u>one</u>?**

a. Do you have any specific changes you would like to make in a curriculum offered in our district?

b. How would you respond to a parent who wants the district to limit access to or remove books from the school library?

c. Who should determine broad educational objectives?

d. How can parents weigh in on the teaching of controversial issues?

e. Which method of teaching reading should be stressed in our district over the next five years?

TRUE-FALSE: Write in TRUE or FALSE for each question. Answer keys are at the end.

_____ 1. It is easier to manipulate the thought processes of a one person than it is to manipulate an entire group.

_____ 2. Morale and psychological factors are often more important than sheer numbers in winning a war.

_____ 3. Deception and surprise are two key principles of battle.

_____ 4. The advice to never "blow your cool" in a controversy means you must be polite and give the other fellow the benefit of the doubt.

_____ 5. The advice by Sun Tzu's _The Art of War_ "to drive the enemy's leaders mad" means to frustrate them into making mistakes.

_____ 6. A psychologically controlled environment makes it easier for the provocateur to frame the debate.

_____ 7. The typical leftist or liberal is careful to study and compare everything our side writes or says so that we are forced to defend our views at every turn.

_____ 8. Political liberals of the eighteenth and nineteenth centuries are operating from the same motives as today's liberals.

_____ 9. When referring to privacy, the term _confidential_ means _anonymous_ in a legal context; the two terms are interchangeable.

_____ 10. People are usually aware of their own belief systems.

_____ 11. Don't count on having a base of support in task forces and other meetings or forums.

_____ 12. Control of the psychological environment helps create a springboard to indoctrination or brainwashing.

_____ 13. Control of the psychological environment determines what topics people discuss and think about and which topics are "off the table."

_____ 14. The "science of coercion" refers to agents of government who monitor airport security lines.

_____ 15. According the Principles of Psych War, the purpose of providing your enemy "an escape route" is to offer him (or her) a false alternative to losing a battle and saving face with constituents.

_____ 16. Slogans help to redefine terms.

_____ 17. If people hear the same phrases and terms often enough, they will start to question their validity.

_____ 18. The purpose of an "academic freedom" clause or policy is to ensure that real academics are taught.

_____ 19. To professional provocateurs, "clarifying the issue" is a delaying tactic to buy time to promote the activity in question.

_____ 20. The term "compelling state interest" is a legal loophole that allows government to break its own laws.

SHORT ANSWER: Finish the sentence with the best response, or answer the question <u>in the space provided here</u>.

General Short Answer:

1. It is harmful to an activist movement if its leaders are confused because . . .

2. Lenient parole laws for violent offenders, politicized and arbitrary child-endangerment laws, and failure to investigate serious offenses like burglary while fixating on minor offenses such as parking and seat-belt violations help create . . .

3. Four key components of psychological manipulation are . . .

4. The difference between a *dictionary* definition and a *working* definition is . . .

5. The difference between *indoctrination* and *desensitizing* is . . .

6. Four of the five basic steps to indoctrination include . . .

7. All warfare is based on _____.

8. One of the most critical aspects of Psych-War, at least for the underdog, is for highly intelligent individual to be able to appear to be stupid, dull, fatigued, and so on. For those who can manage it, why would such capabilities be important?

9. How is it possible to isolate people who are already part of a group?

10. How is it that our adversaries are able to demonize the practice of labeling and stereotyping, yet do it consistently themselves to prejudice the public?

11. How does one keep control of the psychological environment?

12. Every hypothesis (or theory) is based on _____.

13. Appeals work because they are based on . . .

14. In what ways does a facilitator who is under attack try to pass the buck and get parents or the community off his/her back?

15. What does it mean to be told that your criticisms have been taken "under advisement"?

SPECIAL SHORT-ANSWER QUESTIONS

Related to Education, Schools, and Career

1. Why would a psychological "marker" for mental illness include "strong religious belief"?

2. What federal law prevents Information Brokers from combing secure databases for "value and lifestyle" information and cross-matching it with political criteria or other public and private records?

3. Based on this course, what do you imagine "data-laundering" is? (This topic is not covered specifically,)

4. What is the scope of school-related computer cross-matching?

5. What, other than written-down answers to a list of cognitive questions, might function as a "test"?

6. How does "thought disruption" affect learning the classroom setting and post-school careers?

7. What is the most important *ethic* that distinguishes today's school environment from that of the pre-1960s era?

8. What new law institutionalizes mandatory psychological evaluations in schools?

9. What are the long-term effects of psychiatric drugs on growing bodies?

10. What do education experts like Benjamin Bloom consider the primary purpose of education?

ESSAY (non-graded):

<u>Your Task</u>: *Fill in the blanks; answer the questions; and, most of all, decide how the above affair could have been better handled.*

A newspaper editorial described how groups of disenfranchised citizens were brought together to "discuss" what they felt needed to be changed at the local level. A written compilation of these "discussions" influenced a new writing of the city/county charter.

What happened is that the facilitator began by appearing neutral, lulling everyone into a false sense of ownership about the discussion (by calling them _____). She worked the crowd to establish a good-guy/bad-guy role. Anyone disagreeing with the preferred viewpoint ended up appearing as the bad guy, the others as rational and "with it." (What strategy did she use?) This had the effect of sending a clear message to the rest of the task force: Unless they wanted the same treatment (called _____), they best keep quiet. Once the facilitator had managed to identify her opposition, she once again became everybody's pal, and the agenda and direction pursued a predictable course because the majority _____.

Next, attendees were broken up into smaller groups of seven or eight. Each had its own facilitator—taken, of course, from "selected" participants. Each group got a pre-selected "leader," who then proceeded to steer their task force toward certain issues, as no other topics were entertained. Participants were encouraged to put their ideas, and even disagreements, anonymously on a piece of paper, with the results to be compiled "at a later time."

When asked later about how the various responses were compiled, most participants believed that the facilitators took all the concerns and presented both the pros and cons to superiors. A few days later, when some participants asked each other whether what they wrote down was incorporated into the final outcome, the typical answer was: "Well, I wondered about that, because what I wrote didn't seem to be reflected in the final draft. I guess my views were in the minority."

Unsurprisingly, the outcome turned out ***not*** to be reflective of the community's views.

SELF-TEST ANSWERS

MULTIPLE CHOICE:

1. f
2. d
3. b, c
4. c or e
5. a
6. c
7. b
8. a, b
9. a, d
10. d
11. c
12. e
13. f
14. a, c
15. a
16. b, c
17. c
18. d
19. c
20. d
21. a
22. d
23. d
24. a, b
25. a
26. c
27. e
28. b, d
29. b, d, e

30.   e

31.   a

32.   c

33.   d

34.   a, c

35.   d

TRUE-FALSE:

1. F
2. T
3. T
4. F
5. T
6. T
7. F
8. F
9. F
10. F
11. T
12. T
13. T
14. F
15. T
16. T
17. F
18. F
19. T
20. T

GENERAL SHORT ANSWERS:

1.   . . . it helps to destroy morale.

2.   . . . a vicious cycle of resentment and reaction.

3.   . . . redefining, re-directing, marketing, and consensus-building.

4.   . . . that the dictionary definition is the one we commonly understand and refer to in our thinking; whereas, a working definition typically is the one that is hidden and which we have to actually work with to solve anything.

5.   . . . that indoctrination is a more effective way to root out a person's emotional support system and replace it with new values; whereas desensitizing is based more on acclimating and conditioning techniques.

6.   . . . sweeping away the emotional support base; disrupting rational thought with series of confusing images; inserting desired ideas into the vacuum left behind; conditioning the subject via repetition using varied formats; and testing, surveying the subject.

7.   . . . deception.

8.   Because he (or she) can help secure the weaker group members to adopt his (or her) viewpoint, and doing so injects an element of surprise that tends to throw off the facilitator.

9.   When a facilitator or perceived "official" uses peer pressure to pit one faction against the other, or deliberately escalates tensions to draw out a naysayer, most people have a natural tendency to back away from the person being targeted.

10.   Through repetition and slogans, especially using an overwhelmingly friendly media.

11.   By framing the debate.

12.   Assumptions or "givens."

13.   . . . the power of suggestion.

14.   Send the complainant to a different (preferably government) agency, or cite a federal or state law.

15.   Staff intend to ignore you and drag out the process.

ANSWERS to SPECIAL EXAM ON EDUCATION, SCHOOLS, AND CAREER:

1. Because it supposedly implies dogmatism, inflexibility, absolutism and intolerance—all now deemed to be indicative of a mental disorder.

2. No federal law yet prevents database searches and cross-matches. Legal experts can't seem to craft a law that differentiates between legitimate and illegitimate cross-matching.

3. "Data-laundering" means hiring a hacker or other expert to expunge or change existing data surreptitiously, usually to circumvent #2 above.

4. Because nearly all information is computerized, and because most computer systems are now standardized for compatibility purposes, data-transfer and cross-matching are nearly pervasive, even with encryption technology.

5. Sales figures, box-office profits (as from movies), "confidential" polls and questionnaires, and TV-audience share.

6. "Thought disruption," a technique launched in 1940s Germany, as well as "thought disorganization theory," articulated around the same time by Alexander Luria in Russia, both entail series of planned interruptions built into the school day that impede a child's ability to concentrate on anything. It is often mistaken for a "mental disorder," called Attention-Deficit Disorder," for which the child begins a life of prescribed, psychotropic drugs.

7. Interdependence and collective (team) spirit as opposed to independent thinking.

8. Mental-health screening programs (such as "TeenScreen," not covered by name in this course, although it is well-known and typical).

9. Nobody knows, because they haven't been around long enough, but today they are becoming suspect in the growing list of random, mass killings.

10. Transforming social and political attitudes; in Bloom's words: "to change the students' fixed beliefs."

ANSWER to NON-GRADED ESSAY:

First, the easy questions: The facilitator referred to the group as "stakeholders," in order to engage them in the debate. Then, she used the Delphi Technique to create the psychological environment in which she could "push" the view her boss (or client) wanted. Unless they wanted the same treatment (called "marginalization"), they kept quiet. The majority either "capitulated" or "arrived at a phony consensus."

Deciding how the affair could have been better handled by participants, will require brainstorming. There is no single answer. But the bottom line is that the facilitator should have been questioned up front concerning her affiliation, who paid for her services and other queries that would prompt this person to reveal the "preferred," or pre-determined, outcome. In other words, the group should have made the facilitator reveal her agenda before the participants were goaded into revealing theirs and feeling isolated.

OVERALL GRADING SCALE:

All Correct = A+

 1 – 6 incorrect = Fit for public office (A)

 7 – 13 incorrect = Study up for debates (B)

14 – 20 incorrect = Can be manipulated by special interests (C)

21 – 27 incorrect = Not ready for PrimeTime (D)

28 or more incorrect: Frankly, my dear, you're "gonna" get squashed

APPENDIX

School Assessments Versus Real Tests

Over the years I have written a couple of books and given many speeches detailing the differences between assessment-style questions and academic tests. Without going into quite so much detail, what follows is a sampling.

For purposes of comparison, the first example below is an honest-to-goodness <u>test</u>, circa 1875, this one forwarded from Salinas, Kansas. It is not a "questionnaire," not an "assessment," not an "instrument." Notice the construction is not "multiple choice"; comprehensible sentence structure was required. Note also the first entry under Geography: "What is climate? On what does climate depend?" That alone should give our nation's education policymakers a reality check concerning the importance of teaching of basic science to students in the *true* spirit of a multi-disciplinary approach. Following this example, is the Entrance Exam for Jersey City Public High School Students, Circa 1885—again, a real test.

8TH GRADE FINAL EXAM, 1875

Grammar (1 hour)

1. Give nine rules for the use of capital letters.
2. Name the parts of speech and define those that have no modifications.
3. Define verse, stanza and paragraph.
4. What are the principal parts of a verb? Give principal parts of "lie," "play," and "run."
5. Define "case" and illustrate each.
6. What is punctuation? Give rules for principal marks of punctuation.

7–10. Write a composition of about 150 words and show therein that you understand the practical use of the rules of grammar.

Arithmetic (1 hour, 15 minutes)

1. Name and define three Fundamental Rules of Arithmetic.

2. A wagon box is 2 ft. deep, 10 ft. long and 3 ft. wide. How many bushels of wheat will ithold?

3. If a load of wheat weighs 3,942 lbs. What is it worth at .50/bushel, deducting 1,050 lbs. for tare?

4. District No. 33 has a valuation of $35,000. What is the necessary levy to carry on a school for seven months at $50 per month, with $104 for incidentals?

5. Find the cost of 6,720 lbs. coal at $6.00/ton.

6. Find the interest of $512.60 for 8 months and 18 days at 7%.

7. What is the cost of 40 boards 12 inches wide and 16 ft. long at $20 per foot?

8. Find the bank discount on $300 for 90 days (no grace) at 10%.

9. What is the cost of a square farm at $15 per acre, the distance of which is 640 rods?

10. Write an example of a bank check, a Promissory Note, and a receipt.

US History (45 minutes)

1. Give the epochs into which US History is divided.

2. Give an account of Columbus' discovery of America.

3. Relate the causes and results of the Revolutionary War.

4. Show the territorial growth of the United States.

5. Provide a short history of Kansas.

6. Who were Morse, Whitney, Fulton, Bell, Lincoln, Penn, and Howe?

7. Name events connected with the following dates: 1607, 1620, 1800, 1849, 1865.

Orthography (1 hour)

1. What is meant by the following: Alphabet, phonetic, orthography, etymology, syllabication?

2. What are elementary sounds and their classifications?

3. Give examples of each of the following: Trigraph, subvocals, diphthong, cognate letters, linguals.

4. Give four substitutes for caret 'u.'

5. Give two rules for spelling words with final 'e.' Name two exceptions under each rule.

6. Give two uses of silent letters in spelling. Illustrate each.

7. Define the following prefixes and use in connection with a word: bi, dis, mis, pre, semi, post, non, inter, mono, sup.

8. Mark diacritically and divide into syllables the following, and name the sign that indicates the sound: card, ball, mercy, sir, odd, cell, rise, blood, fare, last.

9. Use the following correctly in sentences: cite, site, sight, fane, fain, feign, vane, vain, vein, raze, raise, rays.

10. Write 10 words frequently mispronounced and indicate pronunciation by use of diacritical marks and syllabication.

Geography (1 hour)

1. What is climate? Upon what does climate depend?

2. How do you account for the extremes of climate in Kansas?

3. Of what use are rivers? Of what use is the ocean?

4. Describe the mountains of North America.

5. Identify and describe the following: Monrovia, Odessa, Denver, Manitoba, Hecla, Yukon, St. Helena, Juan Fernandez, Aspinwall and Orinoco.

6. Name and locate the principal trade centers of the United States.

7. Name the republics of Europe and give the capital of each.

8. Why is the Atlantic Coast colder than the Pacific in the same latitude?

9. Describe the process by which the water of the ocean returns to the sources of rivers.

10. Describe the movements of the earth. Give the inclination of the earth.

Entrance Examination for Jersey City High School Students

Circa 1885

As a guest on Pat Buchanan's radio show a few years ago, this author brought along a copy of this test to prove that American schools were not pursuing real academics. A liberal professor represented the opposing view, alleging that the three R's were less relevant today, falling way behind things like teamwork and socialization. Thus, the perfect time to whip out a vintage test from 1885—the "Entrance Exam for Jersey City Public High School Students"! (This test was reprinted in both the *Hudson Dispatch*, Union City, New Jersey, and later in the *Wall Street Journal*, June 9, 1992, Sec. A., p.16. This version is somewhat abridged for the sake of brevity, and a few tiny clarifications appear in brackets for clarification purposes and to conform with up-to-date terminology.) It turned out that neither the liberal professor, nor even Mr. Buchanan (a former Jesuit student), could answer most questions, and we all dissolved into laughter. Here it is, **complete with the actual answers (not "responses"):**

ALGEBRA

1. Define Algebra, an algebraic expression, a polynomial. Make a literal trinomial.

   ANSWERS: Algebra: A method of computation in which letters represent numbers and quantities in order to uncover an unknown quantity. An algebraic expression is an equation consisting of a collection of variables and numbers involving addition, subtraction, multiplication, division, or other kind of calculation. A polynomial: A sum of two or more algebraic equations. An example of a literal trinomial: $x + y + z$

2. (a) Write a homogeneous quadrinomial [i.e., a polynomial with four terms] of the third degree. (b) Express the cube root of 10ax in two ways.

   ANSWERS: (a) $x^3 + 3x^2y + 4xy^2 + 5y^3$

   (b) cube root of $\sqrt[3]{10ax}$ can be expressed as $\sqrt[3]{10ax}$ - or as - 10ax to the 1/3 power –or– $(10ax)^\beta$

3. Find the sum of $3x - 4ay + 7cd - 4xy + 16$, and $10ay - 3x - 8xy + 7cd - 13$.

   ANSWER: Sum: $6ay + 14cd - 12xy + 3$

ARITHMETIC

1. If a 60 days note of $840 is discounted at a bank at 4 1/2% what are the proceeds?

   ANSWER: 365-day year, $833.79

2. Find the sum of {the square root of} 16.7281 and {the square root of} .72 1/4.

   ANSWER: 4.94

3. The interest of $50 from March 1st to July 1st is $2.50. What is the rate?

   ANSWER: 15 percent

4. What is the cost of 19 cwt. 83 lb. of sugar at $98.50 a ton?

   ANSWER: Using US hundred weight of 100 pounds, $97.66.

5. By selling goods at 12 1/2% profit a man clears $800. What was the cost of the goods, and for what were they sold?

   ANSWER: If profit is based on cost, cost is $8,400 and selling price is $7,200. If based on selling price, cost is $5,600 and selling price is $6,400.

6. A merchant offered some goods for $1170.90 cash, or $1206 payable in 30 days. Which was the better offer for the customer, money being worth 10%?

   ANSWER: $1,170.90

GEOGRAPHY

I. What is the axis of the earth? What is the equator?

   ANSWER: The real or imaginary line on which the earth rotates or is supposed to rotate.

2. What is the equator?

   ANSWER: Imaginary circle around the earth that is everywhere equally distant from the two poles and divides the earth's surface into the northern and southern hemispheres;

3. What is the distance from the equator to either pole in degrees, in miles?

   ANSWER: 90 degrees, and 6,250 miles

4. Name four principal ranges of mountains in Asia, three in Europe, and three in Africa.

   ANSWER: Asia: Himalayas, Urals, Hindu Kush and Khangal; Europe: Alps, Carpathians and Pyrenees; Africa: Atlas, Drakensberg and Ethiopian Highlands.

5. Name the capitals of the following countries: Portugal, Greece, Egypt, Persia, Japan, China, Canada, Cuba.

   ANSWER: Portugal: Lisbon, Greece: Athens, Egypt: Cairo, Japan: Tokyo, China: Peking (Beijing), Canada: Ottawa, Cuba: Havana.

6. Name the states on the west bank of the Mississippi, and the capital of each.

   ANSWER: Louisiana (Baton Rouge), Arkansas (Little Rock), Missouri (Jefferson City), Iowa (Des Moines) and Minnesota (St. Paul).

7. Write the state(s) or country [associated with] the following: Detroit, Chicago, Portland, Rio Janeiro, Callao, Venice, Bombay, St. Louis, Halifax, Vera Cruz.

   ANSWER: Michigan, Illinois, Oregon or Maine, Brazil, Peru, Italy, India, Missouri, Nova Scotia, Mexico.

8. Name 10 countries of South America, and the capital of each.

   ANSWER: Argentina (Buenos Aires), Bolivia (La Paz), Brazil (Brasilia), Chile (Santiago), Colombia (Bogota), Ecuador (Quito), Paraguay (Asuncion), Peru (Lima), Uruguay (Montevideo), Venezuela (Caracas).

9. In what countries is coffee raised?

   ANSWER: Tropical countries such as Brazil, Colombia, Venezuela and Nigeria. [Today, one could also add US, because Kona coffee beans are grown in Hawaii.]

10. New York is nearly 75° west of London. When it is noon at the former, what time is it at the latter?

    ANSWER: 5 p.m.

GRAMMAR

1. Analyze the following (ANSWER WILL BE A TYPICAL GRAMMATICAL DIAGRAM FOR MARKUP):

   Perseus ground his teeth with rage, for he saw that he had fallen into a trap.

2. Make a list of all the verbs in the sentence above, and give the principal parts of each of them.

   ANSWER: Ground: *grind, ground, ground*; saw: *see, saw, seen*; had fallen: *fall, fell, fallen.* "Had fallen": past perfect tense of the verb fall; this tense is used to indicate that the action of falling took place at a time before the action of seeing. "Saw": the simple past tense of the verb "to see," used here to indicate a) what caused Perseus' rage, and b) the sequence of events in the sentence.

3. Give two uses of the hyphen.

   ANSWER: To join two words used as a compound noun; to indicate division at the end of a line of type.

4. Copy the sentence below. Punctuate and word it properly. "Will you please to tell me boys, for what the reindeer is useful"?

   Please tell me, boys, for what purpose are reindeer useful?

5. Write a sentence containing a noun used as an attribute, a verb in the perfect tense potential mood, and a proper adjective. ANSWERS WILL VARY.

6. Write four lines of poetry, giving particular attention to the use of capitals, and to punctuation.

[<u>Sample</u> ANSWER follows]
   Had we but world enough and time,
   This coyness, lady, were no crime;
   We would sit down and think which way
   To walk and spend our long love's day.

7. Make three sentences, using the plural of sheep

   ANSWERS: {1} in the nominative case,
                          The sheep are in the meadow.
                  {2} in the possessive,
                          The sheep's wool was carded.
                  {3} in the objective.
                          We sheared all the sheep.

US HISTORY

1. What people settled Massachusetts?

   ANSWER: The English Puritans

   Where did they land, and what was their character?

   ANSWER: They landed at Plymouth Rock, Boston, Mass.; and Providence, R.I. They were strongly religious and believed in predestination, divine omnipotence, and the need to create a holy community that could serve as a model for other people.

2. Name four Spanish explorers and state what induced them to come to America.

   ANSWERS: Ponce De Leon, Balboa, Coronado, Cortez. To conquer and Christianize the inhabitants.

3. What event do you connect with 1565, 1607, 1620, 1664, 1775?

   ANSWERS:
   1565—Pedro Menendez founded St. Augustine, Fla.
   1607—Jamestown settled.
   1620—103 Pilgrims landed at Plymouth Rock.
   1664—British seized New Netherland from Dutch.
   1775—Battles of Lexington and Concord.

4. Name the thirteen colonies that declared their independence in 1776.

   ANSWER: Connecticut, Delaware, Georgia, Maryland, Massachusetts, New Hampshire, New Jersey, New York, North Carolina, Pennsylvania, Rhode Island, South Carolina, and Virginia.

5. Name three events of 1777. Which was the most important and why?

   ANSWER: Battle of Saratoga, Battle of Germantown, Battle of Brandywine; Saratoga was the most important, since British Gen. Burgoyne was stopped in his push southward.

6. What caused the war of 1812?

   ANSWER: Disputes over British interference with American shipping and impressments of American sailors; concern that the British were instigating Indian uprisings; and American land hunger.

7. Who was president during that war?

   ANSWER: James Madison

8. What was the result of it?

   ANSWER: The United States acquired Indian lands in the Southeast and Old Northwest; Spain subsequently agreed to recognize a US boundary extending to the Pacific Ocean; the Federalists were stigmatized as traitors.

9. What form of government was established in 1789?

   ANSWER: A federal system of government

10. Into what three branches was the government divided?

    ANSWER: Executive, legislative, and judicial branches

11. What do the Senate and House of Representatives constitute?

    ANSWER: The legislative branch

12. What caused the Mexican war?

    ANSWER: Disputes between Mexico and the United States over the Texas border and Mexico's refusal to sell California and New Mexico to the United States.

13. What was the result [of the above war]?

    ANSWER: The United States acquired California, Nevada, New Mexico, Utah, and parts of Arizona, Colorado, Kansas, and Wyoming, and established the Texas-Mexico boundary at the Rio Grande River.

Assessment Questions, Circa 1980 (and beyond)

By way of comparison, here are some samples from an "assessment" instrument—this one taken from a 1980s version of Pennsylvania's Educational Quality Assessment (EQA). Questions are reflective of all "assessments" (frequently interspersed among legitimate—but not especially rigorous—academic questions, including various versions of the National Assessment of Educational Progress (NAEP) and some modern-day employee applications.

- I often wish I were someone else. [or] I get upset easily at home. The student checks: [a] Very true of me, [b] Mostly true of me, [c] Mostly untrue of me, [d] Very untrue of me.
- You are asked to dinner at the home of a classmate who follows a religion much different from yours. In this situation I would feel: [a] Very comfortable, [b] Comfortable, [c] Slightly uncomfortable, [d] Very uncomfortable.
- There is a secret club at school called the Midnight Artists. They go out late at night and paint funny sayings and pictures on buildings. I <u>would</u> JOIN THE CLUB when I knew . . . [a] my best friend had asked me to join; [b] most of the popular students in school were in the club; [c] my parents *would ground me* if they found out I joined.

There are many other examples that have circulated in recent years. Some of the more outrageous ones from hail Arizona, Texas and Virginia, most of them "weighted" on the side of political correctness, with extra points given for "preferred" (not "correct") *responses* (not "answers").

The point is, how many kids would even get into high school if they had to take that test from 1885, never mind college? As for the religious roots of our nation, the American Humanist Association, the Aspen Institute for Humanistic Studies, and Americans for Separation of Church and State (among others) might wish to rethink their position in light of question #1 under "History."